BUS

7/6/07

The Taboos of Leadership

"For those of us who have led big companies, we rarely find those on the 'outside' who understand the real challenges of leadership. Tony Smith is one of those rare individuals who has made it his life study to understand what it really takes to lead. This book is filled with insight, strategies, and compelling examples of the challenges we all face as leaders."
—Robert C. Nakasone, CEO, Toys "R" Us (retired)

"Dr. Tony Smith has a unique ability to take the theories and history of leadership and turn them into practical application. His in-depth knowledge and perspective enabled me to understand where my leadership skills were successful, and importantly where they were not. I was lucky to have Tony as a teacher for so many years. He gave me a deep understanding of what motivated people and how I could be most effective, and he has done the same here in this novel book."
—Joseph D. Gutman, former senior managing
director, Goldman Sachs, and managing director,
Grosvenor Capital Management

"Peter Drucker said, 'I observe what is visible, but not yet seen,' and that's what Tony Smith does in *The Taboos of Leadership*. In a world where leadership books all start to sound alike, this one stands out!"
—Marshall Goldsmith, author and editor of over
twenty-two books including *The Leader of the Future*
and *What Got You Here Won't Get You There*

"Tony Smith gives us a refreshing look at the *reality*, not the *rhetoric* of leadership. Great lessons for today's leaders and those who want to be leaders."
—Jerome C. Vascellero, partner, the Texas Pacific
Group, and director emeriti, McKinsey and
Company, Inc.

"My first reaction to this book was 'Oh no, another book by a leadership consultant.' By the time I was halfway through, I thought Tony's years of coaching others has provided him with keen insights into the many strategies needed to address the complex, ill-defined nature of the problems that leaders face. Those issues require adaptive thinking, and in challenging us with facing these taboos, I feel that Dr. Smith was reading my mind. I strongly encourage women leaders to read *The Taboos of Leadership*."
—**Dr. Paula A. Cordeiro, dean, School of Leadership and Education Science, University of San Diego**

"Those who write about leadership are sometimes hesitant to face the truth or acknowledge the messy stuff that fills up a leader's day. . . . Tony hasn't shied away from any of that . . . this may be the first nonfiction book about leadership that I've encountered."
—**From the Foreword, Steven M. Bornstein, CEO, NFL Media, and former president, ESPN and ABC Television**

"In this insightful book, Tony Smith tackles head on tough, controversial issues that are seldom acknowledged and even more rarely discussed. His observations and experiences are very additive to leadership learning."
—**Suzanne Nora Johnson, former vice chairman, The Goldman Sachs Group, Inc.**

"I have had the privilege of listening and learning from a number of 'leadership experts' in my career, and I think Tony Smith is one of the best. This is why I have brought him into every organization that I have led. His provocative insights, counsel, and unvarnished feedback that I have valued over the years are reflected in *The Taboos of Leadership*. A must-read for anyone who is truly interested in the field of leadership."
—**Chuck Griffith, executive director, Arcapita Inc., and former CEO of Ingersoll Dresser**

THE TABOOS
OF LEADERSHIP

JB JOSSEY-BASS

THE TABOOS OF LEADERSHIP

The 10 Secrets No One Will
Tell You About Leaders and
What They Really Think

Anthony F. Smith

Foreword by
Steven M. Bornstein

John Wiley & Sons

Published by Jossey-Bass
A Wiley Imprint
989 Market Street, San Francisco, CA 94103-1741 www.josseybass.com

Jossey-Bass books and products are available through most bookstores. To contact Jossey-Bass directly call our Customer Care Department within the U.S. at 800-956-7739, outside the U.S. at 317-572-3986, or fax 317-572-4002.

Jossey-Bass also publishes its books in a variety of electronic formats. Some content that appears in print may not be available in electronic books.

Library of Congress Cataloging-in-Publication Data
Smith, Anthony F., 1960-.
The taboos of leadership : the 10 secrets no one will tell you about leaders and what they really think / Anthony F. Smith ; foreword by Steven M. Bornstein.
p. cm.
Includes bibliographical references and index.
ISBN-13: 978-0-7879-9582-9 (cloth)
1. Leadership. I. Title.
HD57.7.S645   2007
658.4'092-dc22   2006101888

Printed in the United States of America
FIRST EDITION
HB Printing   10 9 8 7 6 5 4 3 2 1

CONTENTS

FOREWORD BY STEVEN M. BORNSTEIN   xiii

INTRODUCTION   xvii

PART ONE
Introducing the Taboos

1 Taboos and Leadership   3
2 Secret 1: We Know What Leadership Looks Like
   (But We Don't Know What It Takes)   13

PART TWO
Taboos of Persuasion

3 Secret 2: Charisma Shouldn't Make a Difference
   (But It Does)   31
4 Secret 3: Real Leaders Don't Play Politics
   (They Take It Very Seriously)   43
5 Secret 4: Women Make Better Leaders
   (When That's What They Really Want to Do)   55

PART THREE
Taboos of Position

6 Secret 5: The Double Standard Is for Cavemen
   (and the Corner Office)   69

7 Secret 6: Thou Shalt Not Play Favorites with
  Friends and Family (Except When It Makes a
  Lot of Sense)   81
8 Secret 7: A Leader's Fundamental Duty Is to
  Groom a Successor (But It Hurts Like Hell)   91

PART FOUR

Taboos of the Person

9 Secret 8: Leaders Need to Demonstrate Work-Life
  Balance (No Problem; Work Is Their Life)   105
10 Secret 9: Blatant Self-Interest Is Dangerous
  (in Followers, Not Leaders)   119
11 Secret 10: It's Lonely at the Top (But Leaders
  Wouldn't Have It Any Other Way)   129
12 Our Taboos Are Exposed, So Now What?   139

REFERENCES   153
ABOUT THE AUTHOR   155
INDEX   157

To my father, Frank Dominic Smith,
who taught me the transforming power of truth,
and to the many talented leaders I have had
the privilege to serve and who have taught me
more than I could ever have taught them

We should think of leadership taboos in the same way that Nietzsche thought of history:

We wish to use history only insofar as it serves the living. . . . When the historical sense no longer conserves life, but mummifies it, then the tree dies unnaturally, from the top gradually down to the roots, and at last the roots themselves are generally destroyed.

—Nietzsche

FOREWORD

When Tony Smith handed me an advance copy of this book and asked me to say a few words in a Foreword, I told him I didn't read fiction. After I got my laugh in, I took a look at what Tony had done and came away deeply impressed. Leadership books are often filled with theories and ideas that don't feel quite right to those of us actually playing the game. There's a perspective from the sidelines that leadership is neat and tidy and leaders are always in perfect control. Those who write about leadership are sometimes hesitant to face the truth or acknowledge the messy stuff that fills up a leader's day: the egos, the politics, the pure pleasure. In his work and writing, Tony hasn't shied away from any of that. Jokes aside, this may be the first nonfiction book about leadership I've encountered.

Tony has been a special guy in my life for over sixteen years. He was one of the first people I called when I became CEO at ESPN in 1990, and I've brought him into each of the organizations I've been with since, including the NFL. I think he's the best in the business. He doesn't bring pat theories into the boardroom and try to fit the situation to his preconceived ideas. Instead, he has tremendous clarity of thought, an intuitive grasp of what's really going on, and a feel for the emotional aspect of work. I've always looked at leadership as being about managing a team of people. Tony understands how teams work. He knows that they are complex organisms loaded with politics. He points out the real dynamics in simple language, lays out the stakes, and helps me come up with a game plan to win. What more can a leader want in a confidante? Every leader needs one.

Over the course of my career, I've learned a lot about leadership from some truly impressive folks—leaders like Dan Burke and Tom Murphy at Cap Cities and Commissioner Paul Tagliabue at the NFL. I've seen leadership in all its glory and all its rough spots, and I know Tony is right when he says there are things people associated with leadership find uncomfortable to talk about. Take work-life balance, for example. It's politically correct to promote balance, but I've never known any successful leader who didn't eat, sleep, and breathe the job. I suspect most leaders could care less about balance, and it shows. As another example, every leader talks about how important it is to pick a worthy successor, but I've seen how insecurity and ego can get in the way when it comes time to line up someone who's capable of filling your shoes. Some leaders are so insecure they'll surround themselves with inferior people. I've never admired them. They can be witty and charming to be around, but their own ego does them in and hurts their organizations too.

In fact, the role of ego may be one of the biggest leadership taboos I've experienced. When my children ask me what I do for a living, I tell them I spend most of my day managing egos—upward, downward, and laterally. No one talks about that in business school, I bet. To be honest, I haven't expressed that view to many subordinates either, maybe just those I really trust. But essentially that's my job: 98 percent managing egos and 2 percent thinking, all geared around doing whatever it takes to get people to march in the direction I need them to march in. Tony gets that. He understands how big a part pure human ego plays in work and how challenging it is to get a team to come together, focus on common goals, and ultimately win. If I were to boil down the thoughts Tony has expressed in this book and to me personally over the years, they'd all come down to the importance of managing ego: it's the real nature of the game we play.

I do have one argument with Tony's book, however. There's one taboo he didn't mention, and that's luck. Aside from effective management of politics, there's a certain amount of luck involved in being a successful leader. I don't think anybody talks about that, but the truth is, any leader could be pumping gas instead of running a company. Sometimes your best plans go to hell, and you still manage to be the last one standing. We can call that skill or street smarts or panache, but to me we should cut to the chase and acknowledge that it's pure luck.

I feel very lucky at this stage in my career to be working with people I like and respect in a field I truly love. Work demands a lot from people. You spend more time with your colleagues than you do with your families. When you're fortunate enough to find yourself in a situation where you like who you're with and what you're doing, it's easy to give your all. I know Tony feels lucky to work with the CEOs he has been with over the years and to rub shoulders with some of the greatest leaders in the world. His love and passion for the field of leadership shine through clearly in these pages.

You'll learn a lot about the reality of leadership when you read this book. What I respect about Tony above and beyond everything else is that he never brings any agenda to the game. The only thing he wants is your success, and that's why I've brought him into every organization I've worked at. In this book, you'll get that unvarnished perspective Tony is so gifted at providing: no agenda, no baggage, willing to say the things other people aren't able to talk about. I've paid Tony a lot of money over the years for his advice. Now you can pay him a lot less than I have and get his insights cheap.

STEVEN M. BORNSTEIN
CEO, NFL Media

INTRODUCTION

If you only understood . . .

For the past twenty-five years, I've been fascinated with the practical aspects of human behavior, persuasion, and psychology in the setting of the modern organization. That interest has given me the privilege of working closely with leaders—CEOs, top executives, and managers—in corporations all over the world. As a lifelong student of the field of leadership, I am well aware of the number of books already out there that try to shed light on its mysteries. Nevertheless, I believe there's a need for this book.

My first glimpse of this big thing we call a "corporation" or an "organization" came through my dad. He was a truck driver for a major oil company, and when he came home in the evenings, he liked to talk about what had happened during the day. When everything had gone well, Dad had stories that made me think about how wonderful work must be. But on plenty of days, the stories weren't so great. Dad often complained that his boss wasn't treating him well, and he was frustrated with other employees who didn't do their fair share of the work. Usually this was because those employees played the political game so much better, an activity Dad described as "kissing the boss's ass." On far too many evenings, Dad ended up running extra loads and working much longer hours, without extra pay.

Even as a young boy, I remember thinking that if only I could just go to my dad's workplace, sit down with my dad's boss, and talk to him about what was going on, I could make everything better. I wanted to explain to my dad's boss that when he treated my dad poorly, my dad didn't come home happy, and when my dad didn't come home happy, my mom wasn't happy and our whole family felt stressed. I also knew that my dad's performance on the job had to be affected by this treatment. He was a hard worker who never shirked a duty, but I had seen the energy and enthusiasm ooze from him when he was in a good mood and knew that would benefit his company too.

Maybe it's just my makeup, but I never believed that my dad's boss was a jerk. I just figured that he didn't understand the total impact of his approach to managing the team. That desire to intervene, however naively expressed, was a pivotal moment for me. I thought if I could get into the organization and talk to the bosses about how they could treat their employees better, those employees would feel better about their jobs and work harder, and their families would be happier too.

Those feelings stayed with me as I grew up. I plowed through school, studying human behavior, psychology, communication, and business, and I even attended divinity school, where I studied religion and philosophy to better understand the impact of our spiritual beliefs on our behavior. I then was a postdoctoral fellow in anthropology to study how culture, heroes, and artifacts affect who we are. Throughout my schooling, I focused on influence and the art of persuasion to better understand what it is that people say, do, think, or feel that drives and enables others to become more effective at what they do.

Once I'd explored academia as far as I could, I started my own consulting firm, considering myself to be an "employee advocate." Whether functioning as a researcher or consultant, I always went into organizations with my kit of tools and measures thinking about the employee side of the equation. My belief was that if I could survey those employees, figure out how everyone was feeling, then bring those data back to organizational leaders, a great light would go on. Time after time, I found myself saying to executives: "Here's where you're missing the mark. Here's what your employees are not happy about. Here's the gap between what the organization claims to believe in and how you really act through your daily operations."

This approach went on for about ten years. But as I became closer to a number of very impressive CEOs and worked closely with some top senior teams, I started questioning the basic premise of my own beliefs. My characteristic tactic—to collect the data, march into the executive's office, dump the information on his or her desk, and say what he or she needed to do differently—was wearing thin in my own mind because it was not reflecting the organizational reality I was experiencing.

One of the CEOs I'd become close to started pushing back. One day, discussing a morale issue at a particularly difficult time in the organization, the CEO leaned back in his chair and gave me a long look. "What about me?" he asked. "You've told me for years what I need to be doing differently for my employees, but it's starting to feel like marriage counseling and being the only one to be criticized and held accountable. It's got to be a two-way street, doesn't it? Shouldn't the employees hear about what I'm struggling with? If I could fill out a survey, I'd let them know how hard I try to do the right thing. I'd list everything I've given up. And in the comment section, I'd ask them, 'What are you going to do differently to help me?'"

This wasn't a shock; instead, it was confirmation of an awareness that had been growing inside me for some time. We talked about his feelings and came to a realization that a public understanding of them would be beneficial to everyone involved, if politically difficult. "So why don't you try to tell them?" I suggested. I already knew the answer, and the CEO confirmed it. "I'd get killed," he said. "People are not prepared to look at a leader that way. It's too big a risk."

My CEO friend couldn't explain his feelings or reactions to anyone outside his most trusted inner circle because he feared that revealing himself in such a way would undermine his effectiveness. He feared that such a view of reality would be used against him. In other words, he sensed a taboo.

I felt that I had stumbled onto an incredibly important and rarely revealed aspect of leadership. Were there really taboos that no leader could discuss? I started testing my hypothesis in my executive coaching work and found that as soon as I broached the subject, the floodgates opened. "Yes," leader after leader told me. "There are things about leadership I would love employees to understand but can't discuss." One CEO let loose when we talked about complaints of a double standard at the executive level: "I know we talk about balance in our values, but I give fifteen to eighteen hours of my life every single day to this organization. My family's screwed up. I've given up everything to help this firm survive and succeed. And if that means I allow myself a few extra perks or privileges, so be it. I deserve it." Another executive confided in me the true reason that he hadn't promoted a young, ambitious female manager to the executive vice president slot: "The last two women executives quit on me six months into the role. One decided to have a baby, and the other decided that the demands of the job were hurting her family. Do you know what that cost me? I can't afford another setback."

Of course, I recognized in such cases that it would be difficult, if not suicidal, for a leader to be open about the truth. In the first example, the CEO made a convincing argument to me about why he didn't give a damn and why his employees should stop "bitching and moaning." To explain that to them, however, would invite ridicule and disdain. In the second case, the CEO's concerns about the tendencies of his female managers to interrupt their careers for family were perfectly legitimate in an economic and operational sense, but he would have looked like an ogre and opened himself up to a lawsuit if he ever expressed his worries publicly.

Nevertheless, I believed that if somehow those taboos could be traversed and real communication established, a better solution would be found. Leaders are in the business of understanding what their employees think and feel. If employees could learn to see the world from their leader's point of view, maybe that understanding would help them appreciate and support their leader better. Every leader I talked to said that the view was surprisingly different from the top floor. As my dad said, "Funny how your old man got smarter and wiser the day you became a father."

It would be an oversimplification to say that I have been an executive advocate ever since. But in my work and in the work of people in my firm, I encourage employees to learn how to see the problems they blame on their leader from that leader's point of view. "What challenges do you think the leader is going through? How would you see the issue if you were in the leader's chair? What is it that he or she can't discuss that might explain the problems better?" I

have also encouraged leaders to breach such taboos themselves when it is appropriate and possible: "Why don't you
share that with your team or your organization?" When the
time is right and the scope of the experiment is safe, I have
seen remarkable results. Through the medium of simple
human understanding, an organization's alignment, morale,
and performance levels increase dramatically.

Of course, it's never easy, and some of the taboos of
leadership are off the charts in terms of radioactivity. So that's
why I've written this book. By exposing those leadership
taboos on the page and using anonymous examples culled
through my own coaching experience, I hope to bridge the
gap of understanding between employees and leaders.

If only you understood . . .

THE TABOOS
OF LEADERSHIP

PART ONE

Introducing the Taboos

1

Taboos and Leadership

Painful, touchy, intimate, difficult-to-discuss, and politically incorrect taboos of leadership are the subject of this book. By holding them up to the light, judging them for good or bad, exposing their myths, and revealing their underlying truths, I hope to create a helpful and instructive description of leadership that will benefit leaders, their followers, and those who aspire to become one or both.

Why is this necessary? Because leadership is so poorly understood. Despite the billions of dollars that have been spent on leadership development by companies around the world, the results have been mixed. The reason is simple: the biggest taboo of leadership by far is our unwillingness to examine what it really takes to lead. We've expanded the term *leadership* to refer to anyone who is relatively skilled at his or her job, holds a position of some authority, and has a modicum of charisma. We talk about servant leadership, influencing quietly, leading from the heart or by example, or passionate, irreverent, or visionary leadership. We do not talk about the importance of power, intelligence, self-centeredness, political gamesmanship, double standards, insecurity, arrogance, competitive fire, or manipulation. That would be way too much reality for most people's tastes—an experience akin to looking at war photographs on the nightly news and seeing the terrible reality of violence up close. We prefer our leaders, like our movie stars, to be idealized versions of who we want to be.

And yet if we do not understand what leadership really takes, how can we possibly do a better job at identifying, developing, becoming, and coaching leaders? Notice the focus on leadership, not just being a leader. As an intellectual mentor of mine, James MacGregor Burns, stated in his book *Leadership* (1978, p. 2): "The Crisis of Leadership today is the mediocrity of so many men and women in [positions of influence]. The fundamental crisis underlying [this] mediocrity is intellectual. If we know all too much about our leaders, we know far too little about *Leadership.*"

So much has been written about leadership but so little of that writing illuminates what it takes to lead. Do a Web search of leadership, and you will see what I mean. It's nearly as popular as diets, self-help, and cooking. On closer review, though, you will see that most of those leadership books focus on the biography or philosophy of the leader, not on what this person thinks and how he or she makes tough decisions, attains and keeps the position, gains power and uses it, inspires fear as well as loyalty and commitment, or what being a leader costs on a personal level and what it provides in compensation for that loss. Consider how familiar some of these leaders are as household names and yet how little we really know about the leadership they exercise.

Richard Branson, founder of Virgin, transformed the music industry with panache and style, swept into the airline business and did the same, then turned to soft drinks, cell phones, and whatever else struck his fancy. And in his spare time, when he wasn't engaged in the kinds of dalliances that made the scandal sheets happy, he was attempting to be the first person to circumnavigate the globe in a hot air balloon. But what is he really like, what drove him, and what did it take to become so successful? The truth of the matter is that we don't know.

Jack Welch started his tenure as CEO of GE by laying off thousands. At first, he was vilified as Neutron Jack, after the bomb that kills people but leaves structures intact. Next, he became Jack Welch the educator, leading teach-ins at the famous executive education center in Crotonville, New York. Along the way, he set GE on course for its amazing run of success by laying out ground rules that became legendary, like become number one or number two in your market or get out. When he cashed out, people were shocked, *shocked,* at the level and kind of compensation he received. But didn't Jack Welch embody both dimensions; the good as well as the bad, all along?

Herb Kelleher (Southwest Airlines), Bill Gates (Microsoft), Lou Gerstner (IBM), Roberto Goizueta (Coca-Cola), Jeffrey Immelt (GE), Steven Jobs (Apple), Sam Walton (Wal-Mart), Paul Tagliabue (NFL), Mary Kay (Mary Kay Cosmetics), Tom Watson (IBM), Meg Whitman (e-Bay), Michael Dell (Dell Computers), Warren Buffett (Berkshire Hathaway), Larry Bossidy (Honeywell International), and even Donald Trump (Trump Organization) all are legendary figures, and all are poorly understood. We set them on a pedestal for what they have accomplished but do not have the slightest inkling what it took for them to get there. When other leaders experience a fall from grace, we are just as bewildered. Martha Stewart's petty greed cost her company hundreds of millions; Jeffrey Skilling's hubris cost shareholders billions. By labeling such people as aberrations, monstrosities, and bad apples, we do ourselves little good. The explanation may be comforting, but the level of our understanding goes no deeper than a newspaper headline. We can't talk about what makes a leader successful any more than we can talk about what makes this person a villain. Barbara Kellerman's book *Bad Leadership* (2004), for instance, focuses on ineffective and unethical examples and aspects of leadership, not the deep psychological currents that led people in power astray. The entire subject is in itself a taboo.

Taboos are issues or ideas that are too painful, embarrassing, threatening, or complicated to talk about openly. *Webster's Dictionary* defines a taboo as, "a sacred prohibition put upon certain people, things, or acts which makes them untouchable." In daily life, taboos are emotional hot buttons, something we may be attracted to privately but ashamed of publicly. As social beings, we go to great psychological lengths to avoid talking about them openly. Rather than deal with their reality, we prefer to talk about the mask hiding their reality. In that sense, taboos produce myths as much as euphemisms—glamorized falsehoods or false pictures that have the air of truth but none of the substance, the pithiness of wisdom but none of the depth. Taboos can be large or small, major or minor. We use euphemisms, myths, and glossed-over descriptions to cover them up. We don't talk about going to the toilet to evacuate our bowels; we say that we are visiting the bathroom. We don't think about death as a state in which we decay under the ground in a sealed box; we say that someone has passed away and been laid to rest. Indeed, our personal fear of death makes it one of the most difficult of events to contemplate, or as the great minister and sociologist Anthony Campollo puts it, "we can't stand the macabre sound of the grass growing over our own graves." Some of us won't even visit the doctor because we don't want to face the possibility of illness. Rather than confront our fear of death, we'd rather not know, and then it might be too late. Others obsess about illness and fail to live fully because their fear of death has them in an equally powerful grip.

Organizations have cultural taboos. Some have an unwritten, unspoken taboo against leaving work early. Whether your tasks for the day are long finished or too difficult to complete without a good night's rest, the people in such organizations plug away and stay chained to their desks until well past quitting time because it would "look bad" if they left. Some organizations have a taboo against challenging up; in meetings, no one contradicts the boss. Some organizations are okay with office romances or after-hours drinking, and at other organizations, these actions are social violations and cause for dismissal. One midwestern organization prohibits employees from smoking not only inside the workplace but even inside their own homes.

Where do taboos get their power? It's a fascinating question because it gets to the heart of why one thing can be so tantalizing to some and so repellant to others. I believe that taboos are powerful because when we approach one, we touch a nerve. The surprise of the touch can cause us to stop or jump back. It's not easy to recognize when we feel a taboo personally, but sometimes we can see the effect of a taboo in others. Consider the next time someone around you becomes highly emotional, sensitive, titillated, or defensive about something; chances are that person is reacting to a taboo. The attraction or threat is powerful because it goes deeper than the surface level of consciousness. By the time we are adults, we have become adroit at controlling and influencing our feelings and thoughts on the surface. But taboos tunnel deeper than that and strike at the heart of something older, more primitive, and instinct driven: they touch our most innate desires and fears.

In my view, taboos are neither inherently good nor inherently bad. I believe that some serve a legitimate purpose by providing a restraint or social censure on unacceptable behavior. I also believe that other taboos obscure our understanding of important matters and need to be exposed. A *Harvard Business Review* article, "Breakthrough Ideas for 2005" (Buchanan, 2005), even included, as idea number thirteen, "A Taboo on Taboos." But how do we know how far to go? Without mature examination, it's difficult to know which taboos should be kept locked up and which should be defused and disempowered.

In this book, I examine ten taboos of leadership. In my career as an academic, a leadership expert, and a coach and confidante to senior executives, I have encountered these taboos over and over again. They are the deepest, most secretive, and radioactive misconceptions surrounding leadership. I did not choose them because I thought they were good or bad. I chose them because they are taboos. There are certainly many others in leadership, but the ten I've chosen to write about are exemplary of the notion of modern taboos. In the process of thinking and writing more deeply about these taboos, I have come to some opinions about which of them I think are worth preserving and which I think need to be exposed and left behind. That's my judgment, and not all leaders in all circumstances may agree with me. My overall objective is to define what leadership really takes. I believe that if we understand the taboos of leadership clearly, then some of our more wasteful, wrong-headed, and even potentially dangerous misconceptions will be corrected.

For example, the simple idea of hierarchical authority has become a taboo in recent years. Does hierarchy serve a purpose, or is it an impediment to organizational success, as so many currently believe? No one who has ever served in the military would argue that hierarchy—knowing who to turn to for clarity and direction in a crisis—is a bad thing. But is it bad for organizations? Most leaders I know would be reluctant to say that they are fans of hierarchical leadership, even if they believe in its merits. Does hierarchy stifle innovation, debate, dissent, creativity, and personal growth? Or does the fact that we view hierarchy as bad and prefer not to acknowledge its existence lead to bigger problems?

What about office politics? Many think that any form of political gamesmanship is wrong. In an age in which leaders aspire to sincerity and transparency, people should speak from the heart and never disguise an opinion, a feeling, or a worry. If that is so, how come political gamesmanship is such an un-acknowledged aspect of surviving and succeeding in organizational life? Many times, it seems, the people who are most political are the ones who are most successful at rising through the ranks. Is this good or bad? Maybe it's both. In my experience, being political is a critical capability of leadership at all levels, but a certain type of political leadership serves you (and your organization) well on your way up, while a different kind is more suitable, useful, and inspiring at the top. The danger is not that political gamesmanship exists; it is that if we refuse to acknowledge its existence and fail to understand it better, we risk derailing our up-and-coming leaders for skills that they need and undermining our senior leaders for skills that will serve us well. By not understanding the nature of hierarchy, we fail to examine its costs and its benefits.

Why is this such a bad thing? Here's one reason. Imagine that you have an incredible misconception about what it takes to be a medical doctor. You don't know that you need to study intensely for eight to ten years. You don't know that you need to work forty-hour shifts. You don't know that you need to touch dead bodies and examine wounds and talk to people whose relatives are not going to survive. You don't know about hospital inefficiencies or the difficulties of getting paid by health maintenance organizations. You have no idea of the difficulties dealing with insurance companies. As a result of this ignorance, you don't know what emotions you will feel or not feel as you do this work, and you don't know what the rewards and costs will be. Imagine, for example, that you believe the job of being a doctor will require only that you see patients who are somewhat ill in a sanitized visiting room and write them prescriptions on a pad of paper and collect a large paycheck every month while getting in plenty of golf. If you aspire to be a doctor, wouldn't you be better off knowing the truth before you decide whether that role is right for you? Even if you can't fully understand how difficult the job will be, won't you be better off if you've at least been given a snapshot of that reality in advance? If you were a patient, wouldn't you also benefit by understanding a little more clearly what doctoring is all about?

    We don't provide leaders or those who aspire to leadership or even those who follow leaders with any of that truth. Instead, we offer them a sanitized, air-brushed, or glorified picture of leadership that masks or disguises reality. How then do potential leaders know what they are getting into? Is the job within their capabilities, interest, or makeup? Is it something they would want for themselves from a cost-benefit analysis? Leadership is not for everyone, nor should it be. Moreover, there is a danger that all of the scandals that have been surrounding leadership are off-putting for future leaders. An article in the *Wall Street Journal* posed the idea that the "Backlash Against CEOs Could Go Too Far" (2005). In fact, I believe that if up-and-coming leaders see only strife and misery in the role of top executive, they will be moti-

vated to reach the top for one reason only: the money. There
are many, many perks and responsibilities to leadership; without an in-depth, brutally honest, and well-rounded understanding of what the job entails, how can any young person
with high potential know whether he or she even wants to
play the game?

What about today's leaders? Most are unable to acknowledge or examine in the light of day what really motivates
them. They won't face what they dislike or like, what they
fake or disguise. They don't confront the costs or clearly appreciate the benefits of their role. As a result, I believe that
many leaders risk a deep personal strain because of the tension that arises between what they actually know inside and
what they think they need to project to others.

I also believe that a leader's effectiveness is reduced in
the eyes of followers if they do not understand what leadership takes. The existence of leadership taboos creates a gap
between myth and reality. No matter how effectively a leader
performs, any gap between idealized expectation and the
gritty reality undermines credibility.

As you read about the taboos of leadership in this book,
keep in mind that some taboos are functional and others are
extremely dysfunctional. If we do not acknowledge their existence and understand their reality, we are allowing ourselves
to be held prisoner to misconceptions, not unlike those who
believed the world was flat or that life could never be created
in a test tube. Ignorance is no excuse, and it is no virtue. What
we do with our knowledge as mature and rational adults
makes all the difference in the world.

If I startle you, enlighten you, shift your perspective,
confirm some of your deepest suspicions, or make you curious about other leadership taboos, I will have done my job. I

also hope that you enjoy the journey. Reading about taboos and encountering them firsthand are two different experiences. From the safety of distance, we can find even the most difficult things interesting, titillating, and sometimes uproariously funny. Laughter and intrigue are our psychological safety valves, outlets for the release of the pressures of our social mores. Experiencing taboos is part of what make us human. Understanding taboos is part of what makes us wise.

2

Secret 1

WE KNOW WHAT LEADERSHIP LOOKS LIKE (BUT WE DON'T KNOW WHAT IT TAKES)

What does leadership *really* take?

Few people who are not leaders ever ask that question. In fact, it doesn't even occur to them. James MacGregor Burns (1978) wrote, "Leadership is one of the most observed and least understood phenomena on earth" (p. 1). As a society, we have developed a glossed-over and glamorized view of leadership. Our CEOs and senior executives have been mythologized to such an extent that we can no longer see them clearly. Many are heroic, larger-than-life figures, and even the ones we consider villains have been portrayed as epic in scale. A leader's faults are beyond our faults; a leader's virtues are magical and legendary. And yet, paradoxically, we think we can be just like them, achieve what they have achieved, climb the mountains that they have climbed, by learning more about them as people. In other words, we have confused the act of leadership with the biography of the leader.

Ask a leader what leadership really takes, and you will not learn much. Few have any desire to address the issue publicly and honestly. The truth is too touchy and intimate, too painful and politically incorrect—too filled with taboos. Talking about what leadership really takes is like talking about sex, money, politics, or an intimate health issue. In the company of other leaders—those who know—the discussion could be interesting, enlightening, helpful, even affirming. But a leader would never speak openly about the concerns, drives, desires, enjoyments, fears, likes, and dislikes of leadership in front of someone who has not experienced that reality directly. It would expose too much, make him or her seem too monstrous, ambitious, insecure, arrogant, calculating, and crassly motivated. It is better to be misunderstood and thought of in idealized and glamorous terms than to be seen in close-ups—with blemishes and scars in stark view.

We used to view leadership (the act, not the science) as a means to an end. The leader's skills, personality, experiences, and passions are all focused on the task of making the organization better, stronger, and more profitable. At some point, however, we also started to analyze how that alchemy works and make up a lot of theories to explain leadership the science. Today, leadership development is a billion-dollar industry. Critics could even say that developing leaders is no longer a means to an end; it has become an end in itself.

Despite all of the effort we have put into explaining leadership, I believe that we still don't understand its true nature. In our attempts to create formulas and answers, we have invented sanitized and stylized theories. As a result, we have developed a tendency to overlook what leaders actually do and why they do it. Part of the problem in that regard is that we are afraid to look too closely at the dark or gritty side of leadership—those aspects that feel right to the leader but look wrong to the public. Unfortunately, that lack of clarity makes it difficult to meet the objectives we hope leadership development can accomplish. We end up designing leaders who look great in the classroom or in the case study but would, without their other instincts and urges, lack something in the real world. Conversely, leaders who are successful never quite fit the theories we apply to them and are always messier and more complex than we would predict.

As the great leadership scholar Joseph Rost (1991) has said, "Leadership is a word that has come to mean all things to all people" (p. 7). We fling it around whenever we want to describe someone making something happen relatively independently or serving as a role model for others. We don't like to discuss leadership in the context of followers, and we don't like to take a hard look at what a leader must do to influence others to act in line with his or her agenda or vision. In polite society, we don't talk about a leader's exertion of power, ego, or blatant self-interest. We don't like to discuss what it means to be a follower either. After all, aren't we all leaders in different ways?

Not in my book.

Leadership is a distinct act with distinct outcomes. To understand it better, let's take a brief sidestep into the history of leadership development and see where we pop out in the end.

A BRIEF HISTORY OF LEADERSHIP

Leadership as a science has been around for much of the past one hundred years. The iterations, even from the earliest days, have provided insights that influence how leaders think and behave and how they are perceived and understood. Although no systematic grand theory has been proffered, we have seen a number of ideas that hold to a pattern. If there is a mountain of understanding we are trying to climb, we have been making progress with a series of switchbacks, focusing on the leader as an individual, then on leadership the process, back and forth, up and up. Because of that back-and-forth progression, you might be surprised how the ideas of eighty years ago still influence our thinking today.

Group theory, prominent in the 1930s and 1940s, was the first exploration of leadership. It was based on the idea that leaders don't lead individuals; they actually lead groups. Through studies of group behavior and group psychology, researchers discovered that people act and react differently in groups than they do as individuals and that group dynamics are critical for organizations. Firms like Ford and GE are composed of divisions and departments that are simply groups within groups. The better a person can lead and manage groups, the more effective he or she will be at leading or managing a company. It's an idea that makes a lot of sense intuitively. Today, we rely on group theory whenever we talk about leading teams, one of the buzzier buzz phrases of the past ten years.

In the 1940s, we began to think about leadership in a different way—not so much about what a leader does to manage a group, but what traits a leader has that enable him or her to do so effectively. In other words, we made the transition from the psychology of the group to the psychology of the individual. In the process, we went from an assessment of the external world, where the leader is a dominant actor, to an assessment of the leader's internal world, where he or she is a collection of characteristics. Behind trait theory there is a premise that no matter how well a leader understands groups, teams, and organizations, if that person doesn't have the right traits, he or she will not be effective. Another hypothesis holds that effective leaders have similar traits. They seem, for instance, to be dynamic, aggressive, and confident. This view plays easily into mythical impressions of leadership, also known as the great man theory: both Napoleon and George Washington were great leaders because they were vigorous and decisive men of action. There is a problem in that perspective, however, in that understanding the leaders' traits never really explains how they push their agendas forward. Indeed, confusing the biography of the leader with the act of leadership is a trap we still fall into today.

Instead of concentrating on psychological makeup, we realized that we could understand leaders better if we looked at what they actually do when acting as leader. Social scientists called this the study of behavioralism. By the 1960s, leadership development theory latched on to that idea and began to look at how leaders behave on the job. It was readily apparent that certain behaviors, independent of a leader's psychological makeup, help leaders be successful. It followed that we could seek out future leaders by examining candidates who exhibited those behaviors in other settings or train the leaders we had to exhibit those behaviors more frequently or emphatically.

Behavioralism was a kind of a bridge between the leader's internal world and the impact he or she has on others. The problem with behavior theory was that it was too set in stone. Using behavior theory, we could declare that great leaders are great motivators, teachers, listeners, and decision makers. But we didn't acknowledge the truth that not all leaders are all those things all the time. In fact, effective leaders behave differently in different situations. They adjust their skills and approach and do whatever is necessary to influence others and accomplish their goals.

The idea that leaders act differently according to the situation was labeled situational or contingency leadership theory. This approach shifted the leadership focus resolutely back to the external world again. We discovered that under some circumstances, it's necessary for a leader to be a great motivator and a decisive person of action. But in other circumstances, the leader might need to function as a great teacher or listener. The leader's behaviors, in other words, are contingent on followers' needs.

Situational leadership taught us that leadership is a process, focused on outcomes. But what kind of outcomes really matter? Obviously a successful leader is one who obtains the best possible outcomes, so why not focus on excellence? Leadership excellence theory arose in the 1980s to explore how leaders promote top performance, or excellence, in their organizations. For some people, the idea that leadership is about winning and being number one might have seemed too crass and oriented to the bottom line. No doubt those people were trampled or pushed aside by others rushing forward to embrace the theory. After all, wouldn't a shareholder or even an ambitious employee want a leader who is determined to engage the organization in a relentless search for excellence?

In their book, *In Search of Excellence* (1982), Tom Peters and Robert Waterman noted that great leaders who focus on excellence strive to build organizational cultures that perpetuate excellence. (It is interesting to note that many of the companies profiled in their book have toppled from the top in terms of industry standings.) Around the same time, Terrence Deal and Alan Kennedy, in their book *Corporate Cultures* (1982), showed how organizational cultures are connected to core values, an idea further developed by Jim Collins and Larry Porras in their book *Built to Last* (1997). According to Collins and Porras, great companies, meaning those that outperform their competition over a sustained period of time, are value based. The founders of such companies instill those values, and succeeding leaders foster those values, articulate the organization's vision according to those values, run the company by making all decisions based on those values, and as stewards safeguard those values. According to value theory, leaders needn't worry about their own traits or behaviors, so much as they should be concerned about how well they live and lead by their organization's values.

Where do all these different leadership theories leave us today? If you are not certain, then you are not alone. If I were to tell you that great leaders are effective at leading groups, have specific traits, demonstrate certain behaviors in the right circumstances, and act in ways that show they are cognizant of their organization's culture and values, I'm sure you would have no argument. But does it really explain what leaders do? More important, does it even begin to capture that elusive mix of energy, personality, and circumstance that seems to catalyze the world around the leader?

I don't think we've gone deep enough yet. The theories that we rely on to explain leadership are safe and sanguine. And yet there is little about leadership that is safe and sanguine. Leaders are not easy to be around. They often have difficult personalities, with impossible demands, abrasive rough edges, a relentless sense of drive, blind spots, and dark sides, in addition to all of their wonderful qualities, such as an ability to make things happen, to create and build, to push ideas and products toward profitability, to motivate, inspire, and teach. But focusing only on the positives, while overlooking everything that makes a leader difficult, is a bit like orbiting high above a planet, unwilling or unable to land.

The rough stuff, I call the taboos—those sensitive nerve endings that leaders and followers touch by accident all the time and immediately pull away from. I believe that such places are critical to understanding leaders. But since the theorists, researchers, and teachers are not able to see those areas and the biographers and leaders themselves are unwilling (or would be unwise) to talk about them openly, to whom should we turn to get the real information? In my opinion, the people who understand leadership at its most elemental (both ugly and awe inspiring) are the executive coaches, a group that is now coming into its own.

EXECUTIVE COACHING: PERSONALITY, SITUATION, AND GROUP

For at least the past twenty years, we've had a generation of people who have gotten paid to work closely with leaders on the areas that have an impact on their effectiveness most directly. Usually this isn't about the hard skills of thinking strategically or making decisions; instead, it's about the softer side of leadership. Coaches help leaders assess situations and people and work with them on approaches designed to have maximum organizational impact.

In the process, coaches see leadership up close and personal, in all its glory and all its warts. I've learned how leaders view the world and witnessed the gap that exists between that perspective and how followers view leaders. While I rely on intellectual theories about leadership as tools or frameworks, I find that what really matters is helping a leader work through all of the messier aspects of leadership—those issues that seem right to the leader but look bad to the public—for instance, having to fire someone after he has taken a top job and moved his family across the country, telling a top performer that she is a terrible manager of people, or bringing in a new young star to manage a long-term, very loyal older employee.

In my view, leadership is a process whereby a leader pursues a vision by intentionally seeking to influence others and the conditions in which they work, so that they can perform to their full potential for as long as they possibly can. All of that effort is done in the context of helping the organization realize the leader's vision while also contributing to the personal development of everyone involved. What leadership style and approach is right for a particular situation? In some situations, for example, a caring boss is effective. But at other times, a forceful, demanding, and even manipulative boss has tremendous impact (although there may be long-term costs and benefits to consider in either approach). No one approach is right for every leader in every circumstance. Instead, an effective coach focuses on what leaders need to do to push forward their agenda while helping others realize their potential.

Without a process-oriented approach, it's difficult to be objective about the leader's personality and the associated taboos of leadership. Even trained professionals can be overly enamored or overly exasperated by the leader as a person. Moreover, there are many things that leaders do that others couldn't get away with and can't understand. By treating the taboos of leadership objectively rather than as hot buttons to avoid at all costs, I can sit back and assess their impact. What's going on here? Why does this bother people so much? What's it doing for the leader? How is it harming or benefiting this person in the pursuit of his or her leadership agenda?

Looking at the process of leadership, not the personality of the leader, we can see leadership from three critical vantage points: the arenas in which the leader intersects with followers, with the organization, and with his or her own self.

All three arenas are rife with taboos, but I've chosen those that I believe are particularly timely and controversial. I call them the taboos of persuasion, position, and the person.

TABOOS OF PERSUASION

Leadership is an ongoing or episodic process that is intentional, but getting to the intended goal requires using influence and persuasion. We used to call that "power," but that's a word we now avoid, for complicated reasons.

Influence used to be largely a function of position. Today, our understanding of the process of leadership veers away from the ideas of positional power, authority, manipulation, and coercion. Instead, we now believe that influence happens when leaders use their credibility to have an impact on people and the conditions in which they work. Real leadership, in other words, occurs when followers choose to follow their leaders because those leaders are credible.

The research that our firm, LRI, has conducted suggests that credibility is based on six dimensions—what I call the Six Cs:

Conviction: The passion and commitment the leader demonstrates toward his or her vision

Character: Consistent demonstration of integrity, honesty, respect, and trust

Care: Demonstration of concern for the personal and professional well-being of others

Courage: Willingness to stand up for one's beliefs, challenge others, admit mistakes, and change one's own behavior when necessary

Composure: Consistent display of appropriate emotional reactions, particularly in tough or crisis situations

Competence: Proficiency in hard skills, such as technical, functional, and content expertise skills, and soft skills, such as interpersonal, communication, team, and organizational skills

Followers allow themselves to be influenced to the extent that they view the leader as credible. The catch-22, however, is that leaders do not always gain their credibility through enlightened means. In that gap between theory and practice, executive coaches encounter many taboos. Chris Argyris (1977), the great organizational theorist, labeled this phenomenon "theories in use" versus "espoused theories."

First, we're taught that charisma shouldn't matter. Leaders are not supposed to be movie stars or anointed royalty. Their sense of authority shouldn't need any tricks. In reality, however, highly effective leaders often have a great deal of charisma or magnetism. As an influence tactic, charisma is powerful stuff—a drug that we don't like to admit we need. More important, why is it that we're afraid of charisma? And why do leaders cultivate it deliberately?

Second, some researchers proclaim that the leader should be an open book—a completely accessible figure who wears vulnerabilities on his or her sleeve and shares doubts without fear of losing the respect of others. It sounds nice in theory, but in reality, power, manipulation, and political gamesmanship are critical to effective leadership. How does a leader reconcile that with the intense spotlight thrown on him or her constantly?

Third, we've been taught that in the knowledge economy, where hierarchies have been flattened and networking is key, women make more effective leaders than men. Is there

a gender bias to leadership? Is the bias what we would expect, or are we more influenced by politically correct views
of leadership than we realize?

The chapters in Part Two discuss and analyze these taboos.

TABOOS OF POSITION

There is a reason that the leader is not just the person sitting
in the next cubicle. We adorn our leaders with the status and
trappings of position. And yet much leadership work today is
about dissolving the barriers between levels in an organization. Current theorists talk about there being "leaders at all
levels." We even hold that leaders need to be more humble,
more collaborative and communicative—more like us—than
the traditional figurehead on the top floor.

Nevertheless, a fundamental truth gets in the way of
such an ideal view. Leaders actually need to reduce or remove
doubt in their followers. In fact, that may even be why the
more intimidating trappings of position exist: our fear of the
boss is like the totems or masks that create awe in us and
thereby remove our uncertainty.

Moreover, although we believe that leaders are supposed
to be collaborative and collegial, employees still consistently
give a different message. They want more direction, guidance,
influence, and objective setting from their leaders, not less. As
any honest observer can note, productive and competitive
organizations are characterized by strong, confident leadership. On the one hand, we say that leaders are not supposed
to have all the answers. On the other hand, we are not confident in the direction of our organizations unless leaders act
as though they know where the organization should be

going, what it will encounter along the way, and what the destination will look like once it has been reached. These inherent contradictions point to three more taboos.

First, leaders are supposed to always walk the talk. "Do as I say, not as I do" no longer flies anymore. Yet leaders are drawn to privilege and the trappings of status, and followers gain confidence in leaders who exhibit the confidence of status. No wonder there's a conflict between what we expect from leaders as figureheads and what they and we actually want.

Second, organizations are supposed to be meritocracies now, but we see that favoritism still rules the roost. Does favoritism have an undiscovered function, or is it merely a holdover from a darker age? Why do so many leaders put more emphasis on comfort and familiarity in their circle of key associates than they do on pure talent and performance? Are they blind to the truth, or do they have other needs in mind?

Finally, leaders are no longer supposed to be identified with their organizations in any legacy sense. Founders aside, the leader's position in an organization is meant to be a temporary one, held in trust for the greater good. Why then do so many leaders have difficulty handing over their position or status to a successor? Can leaders identify the best successor on their own, or are they incapable of clearly seeing what's best? For most leaders and most organizations, succession is a danger zone that has many hidden traps.

TABOOS OF THE PERSON

Very few of us understand what it is like to lead. We don't know the responsibilities; we don't feel the pressures; we can't imagine the rewards or the costs.

The work-life balance conundrum is just one pressure point that leaders experience and the rest of us find somewhat baffling. More than most other people in the organization, leaders seem incapable of getting balance right. And yet, ironically, they are supposed to be role models for their followers. Followers look to leaders for an understanding of the boundaries of acceptable behavior. Leaders know no boundaries when it comes to the line between work and life. The leader's perceived lack of balance is a huge issue of tension in today's organization. It is also an entry point to understanding more clearly what motivates and drives leaders and how they view life and work.

We also believe that leaders should be servants of the organization. We no longer consider them monarchs; rather, we see them as stewards, putting aside their own needs for the greater good. Too often in reality, however, leaders disappoint in this regard by demonstrating some kind of behavior that gets viewed as narcissistic, ego driven, or selfishly motivated. What gives? The truth is that few people in any system, let alone a capitalist system, are motivated to devote their talents, energy, and efforts to the greater good at their own personal expense. It's just not human nature. The "genius of capitalism," as former Treasury Secretary Paul O'Neill once put it in a television interview, is that blatant self-interest often intersects with and supports the interest of the greater good. Nevertheless, that doesn't mean that blatant self-interest is beautiful or inspirational to behold.

Fortunately for us, leaders aren't motivated to become leaders by their desire to be noble and worthy. They have other, deeper, much more craven urges to satisfy, including the urge for power, status, and money. What are the costs of craven self-interest? Do leaders understand those costs before they act, or do they bump into the negative perceptions after it's too late?

Most leaders are not prone to self-reflection. They don't live in the past and don't like thinking about mistakes. They're doers, not dwellers. But eventually the doing stops. When a run at the top ends, the leader can feel the loneliness of leadership keenly. Is being a leader worth it? When is enough enough? Perhaps we should know, or at least recognize, the risk-reward ratio of leadership a little better before we judge our leaders, or decide to become one ourselves.

LEADERSHIP IS MESSY

There's nothing tidy or clean about leadership. It's messy, but so is the rest of life.

What makes an effective leader is a contradictory collage of motivations and drivers, rewards and costs. We can't teach leadership, not in the sense that we've been trying thus far. We can't look at all the theories of leadership and say: Do this, this, and this, and you will become or create a good leader. But we can understand leadership much better than we do now. If we take a look below the surface, into the blood, guts, and pulsing arteries of leadership, we are bound to understand leadership as process much, much better. In doing so, we might even come to understand the leader as a person, too.

Are you ready to take a look?

PART TWO

Taboos of Persuasion

Secret 2

CHARISMA SHOULDN'T MAKE
A DIFFERENCE (BUT IT DOES)

Charisma is at a low point in current views on leadership. We're somewhat distrustful of charismatic authority figures today, perhaps equating a leader's charm and oversized personality with the kind of snake oil salesmanship that typified the worst of the late 1990s stock bubble. After Enron, AIG, and Tyco, who can blame us?

There has always been a sense that charisma can be dangerous. Sure, we find charismatic leaders appealing, but can our base instincts to follow someone blindly be trusted? There have been plenty of charismatic leaders in history whose desires have been destructive. Hitler had charisma. So did Charles Manson, the cult figure responsible for the grisly mass murders in the late 1960s. Barbara Walters, after interviewing Manson in prison, claimed that she felt almost compelled to follow the man anywhere; his charisma was that powerful. Undoubtedly there's a dark side to charisma worth being wary about. No wonder that it makes it onto our list of leadership taboos.

The academic position against charisma was articulated particularly well by Jim Collins in his excellent book, *Good to*

Great (2001). In describing companies that had made the leap from good to great, Collins and his research team found that such companies were run by "Level 5" leaders: "Level 5 leaders are a study in duality: modest and willful, humble and fearless" (p. 22). He characterized them as often modest, shy, introverted, and awkward. They "never wanted to become larger-than-life heroes. They never aspired to be put on a pedestal or become unreachable icons. They were seemingly ordinary people quietly producing extraordinary results" (p. 28). Indeed, the only remarkable feature of their lives, outside their accomplishments, was an early formative experience, often life threatening, that seemed to put them into closer contact with core values or a sense of larger meaning. Furthermore, according to Collins, one of the reasons that few companies make the leap from good to great is that most organizations believe that "larger-than-life, egocentric" leaders are necessary. In other words, charisma isn't just unnecessary for great leadership; it's a detriment.

I know a few Level 5 leaders, some of them well. George Bodenheimer, president of ESPN and ABC Sports, is one of the most effective and capable leaders I've encountered. He was labeled the most powerful man in sports by *Sporting News*. He is beloved by his employees as a humble man, in part because he started in the mailroom. But charisma is also part of Bodenheimer's impact on people, and I have known few successful leaders without a healthy dose of it. Collins's view of humble versus charismatic leadership has become de facto conventional wisdom. Since Enron, there has been an undeniable appeal to down-to-earth, stick-to-the-knitting, and (most of all) serious leadership. But I think that while Collins's assertions say some important things about how leaders achieve their effectiveness, he is missing some nuances about what makes leaders compelling. It's hard to argue against the charisma of some of our most heralded and successful leaders, inside and outside business. Gandhi had charisma; so did Martin Luther King Jr., Mother Teresa, Winston Churchill, and Ronald Reagan. These people were known as leaders because of their vision, conviction, and tremendous influence over others, as well as their appealing mystique. In business, few leaders have been as notable as these public figures, but those who transcend their organizations are often undeniably intriguing. Whether Jack Welch, Richard Branson of Virgin, Herb Kelleher of Southwest, or Warren Buffett of Berkshire Hathaway, we want to know more about them, and we want to know more about the secrets they possess. We are drawn to them and want to be more like them.

Let me state flatly: charisma plays a critical role in who we come to see as having leadership qualities. People who are impressive have special qualities. Some of that impressiveness has to do with technical competence, but there is also the impressiveness that comes with good looks, communication skills, or aura. I heard a speaker a few years back cite a study that revealed that 85 percent of Fortune 500 CEOs are male, are above average in height, and tend to be perceived as good looking. Granted, I was unable to confirm this finding, and the changes at the CEO level in the past few years has been significant, but my impression is that this statistic is more accurate than not. Societal norms as to what is or is not leadership play an undeniable part in those we choose to elevate as leaders. Those norms can shift dramatically depending on times and circumstances. What was appealing in one era may be less appealing today. The basic urge to elevate somebody into a leadership role, however, is a biological instinct, rooted

in our need for survival: we're looking for direction, guidance, security, and emotional identification. We may prefer to
deny that urge or sanitize it for public consumption, but it's
a powerful force nonetheless.

WHAT WE'RE LOOKING FOR IN LEADERS

There's a rationale to charisma—one that explains why we
choose the leaders we do. The first part of that explanation
has to do with our desire to identify with our leaders. In
general, we tend to follow or be influenced by those with
perceived similarities to ourselves. Psychologists call this
homophily. At its most basic, homophily can refer to an identification with physical characteristics. If you are tall, male,
and white, you tend to identify with leaders who are tall,
male, and white. If you are female, African American, and
over fifty, you tend to identify with leaders who are also female, African American, and over fifty. Of course, identification can go deeper than physical attributes. If you have a
southern accent and enjoy hunting, chances are you will identify more strongly with a political leader who also hails from
the South and supports gun ownership. If you have strong
religious convictions, you feel more comfortable being led by
someone who is also religious.

Perceived similarity is one aspect to leadership identification, but so is perceived difference. We are not necessarily looking for our leaders to be absolutely like us; we also
hope that they have some differences. Those dissimilarities,
however, should be positive ones—what's known as *optimal
heterophylly.* We hope that our leaders are smarter than we are,
more competent, more visionary, and more articulate. We

want them to be like us at a core level, but better than us too. We are drawn to leaders we can look up to and idealize.

Political consultants monitor these two variables closely. When consultants poll voters to determine which candidate they are most comfortable with, they are essentially asking whom they identify with most strongly. When they ask voters which candidate embodies a critical value like strength, integrity, or virtue, they are assessing the degree of idealization. Similarly, if the leader of your organization articulates values that you embrace and a vision that you share, chances are that you are open to being highly influenced and directed by that person. You feel that this person is like you at some basic level, but also capable of directing you to a place you could not get to by yourself.

THE MYSTIQUE FACTOR

There's a third aspect of charisma: the idea of mystique. Charismatic leaders are people who are both like us and better than us, but they are also a bit mysterious or intriguing. There's something about them that we can't fully grasp or ever know. That unknowable quality beckons us to try and learn more. Picture a cat in the backyard that hears a rustling behind a bush. It stops and waits to hear the sound again. Curious, it pokes behind the bush and becomes more engaged and focused. Intrigue or mystique is a powerful aspect of the charisma taboo, a lure that draws us in.

In order to understand something as shadowy as leadership mystique, it helps to picture leadership in a developmental model that I developed a few years back. Table 3.1 shows the journey an individual takes to compelling leadership:

Table 3.1. The Multifactor Leadership Model

Leadership Role	*Behaviors*
Facilitator: Skill building, developmental	• Asks insightful questions • Solicits input from others • Synthesizes effectively • Gets people involved • Listens well • Facilitates open communication • Promotes constructive debate • Demonstrates empathy • Embraces diversity of all employees • Admits mistakes • Effectively assesses skill and motivation of others
Teacher: Skill building, developmental	• Explains things effectively • Is effective at using analogies and metaphors • Is a good storyteller • Provides effective orientation for new assignments and tasks • Provides appropriate amount of detail • Provides constructive feedback • Encourages learning • Effectively teaches people new skills • Builds understanding • Role-models high standards • Demonstrates commitment to self-improvement
Pragmatist: Skill building, developmental	• Is decisive • Prioritizes well • Demonstrates effective analytic skills • Is bottom-line oriented • Avoids wasting time • Delegates effectively • Plans work effectively • Knows the business • Utilizes resources effectively

Leadership Role	Behaviors
Motivator: Will building, inspirational	• Creates excitement about work • Communicates with optimism • Demonstrates belief in you • Maintains composure in tough situations • Demonstrates passion and conviction • Provides recognition • Is courageous • Inspires people to perform • Is committed to winning • Strives to improve people's performance from "acceptable" to "excellent"
Visionary: Will building, inspirational	• Clearly articulates the end goals • Identifies opportunities before others do • Anticipates change well • Recognizes patterns others may not see • Thinks out of the box • Establishes common purpose • Is innovative • Connects the dots for people (explains how things work together and affect each other) • Understands industry trends well • Sees the big picture
Mystic (magnetism): Will building, inspirational	• Is interesting and intriguing • Appears to have varied interests outside work • Approaches things differently from others • Consistently comes up with unique perspectives • Possesses personal presence • Commands attention when speaking • Is charismatic • Creates a culture of pride • Is self-aware • Is fun to work with

The first three stages of this leadership model—facilitator, teacher, and pragmatist—are technical and can be taught. A young, emerging leader, ambitious to run the company one day, would do well to follow this path. As a low-ranking employee, he or she would benefit from asking insightful questions; engaging with peers, customers, and mentors;, showing emotional intelligence; and demonstrating rudimentary leadership. Once that aspiring leader has gained a certain level of technical and leadership competence, he or she typically demonstrates his or her capabilities by sharing the benefits of this learning with others: explaining things to others, rising to the challenge during teachable moments, helping others build skills, and role-modeling high standards. Finally, to be an effective manager, the young leader becomes a pragmatist, showing decisiveness, bottom-line orientation, efficiency, and effectiveness.

To be effective as a leader, however, an individual must demonstrate some capabilities as a motivator or visionary. A motivator is a leader who is driven for results and aims to bring out that drive in others through support or coercion. In other words, motivation is a transactional activity. A leader tries to improve performance levels in peers and reports by offering carrots (raises, promotions, other rewards) or sticks (punishment, fear of failure, fear of disapproval).

Next on the scale, a visionary is able to see connections and possibilities that others miss, communicate those effectively as desirable future states, and inspire a sense of common purpose in achieving that future.

Charismatic leaders add the elusive quality of magnetism or intrigue to the mix. When they have mystique, there's a force to them. They have a high degree of personal presence. They command attention through exceptional verbal or

nonverbal communication styles. Their way of looking at the
world is unique, and they create an environment that is excit-
ing, fun, or inspirational to be around. They seem larger than
life, and we are always curious and interested in learning
more about them.

Not all successful leaders have mystique as a natural
quality. If we were to meet Bill Gates at our neighborhood
coffee shop, for example, I doubt that we would find him to
be exceptionally interesting or intriguing. The level of mystique that he does have relates primarily to his accomplishments and does not seem to exude from his person. In
contrast, the legendary CEO of Southwest Airlines, Herb
Kelleher, seems to cultivate mystique deliberately. He works
and plays harder than ordinary mortals, outdrinking, out-
smoking, and having more fun than the people around him.
He has tattoos on his biceps and wears Elvis costumes to company parties. He once settled a major legal dispute through
an arm-wrestling competition. His antics, his personality, and
his sense of group mission make him a unique personality
whom others want to emulate and please. Winston Churchill
is another leader who had mystique. His eloquent speeches,
bold pronouncements, decisive depictions of the future, and
deeply considered ideas made him seem a giant. Others
relied on his strength, clarity, and resolve when they could
find it nowhere else. Seeing leadership close up only high-
lights the importance of charisma. The famous turning point
in the Nixon-Kennedy race for president occurred during
the televised debates. Richard Nixon, pale, weary, and sporting a five o'clock shadow, looked less like a leader next to the
tall, youthful, tanned, and athletic-looking John F. Kennedy.
At the end of the debate, television watchers overwhelmingly
selected Kennedy as the winner, while radio listeners thought

that Nixon had done the better job. Kennedy won the election, in no small part because of his charismatic appeal. His leadership legacy lives on because of his mystique.

Mystique is a transformational quality rather than a transactional one. It affects our internal rather than our external state. The values and beliefs of followers of a mystic leader have been changed because of their contact with the leader. Transactional leaders who rely on carrots and sticks to move followers lose their power when they are no longer in positions of authority or influence. But transformational leaders establish a sense of leadership beyond the managerial or supervisory role. They are able to get people to do things that nobody else can.

MANUFACTURING MYSTIQUE

Can mystique be cultivated deliberately? I believe that it can be amplified, but it must also be genuine. A leader cannot simply begin to dress, talk, or act differently in order to convey an aura of mystique. That would be cause for mockery. Instead, he or she develops a sense of mystique naturally or organically, in tune with a greater understanding of life's own mysteries.

When Jim Collins wrote about Level 5 leaders, he mentioned that many had a "formative experience" that had an impact on the direction of their lives. Abraham Zaleznick wrote about the same phenomenon in *The Managerial Mystique* (1989). He said that "leaders grow through mastering painful conflict during their developmental years, while managers confront few of [those] experiences" (p. 5). I believe such an experience is a common ingredient in mystique. Leaders with mystique have often been shaped and inspired by traumatic events such as an accident, the loss of a loved one, or a trying period. The impact seems to raise self-awareness, cause questioning or reflection, deepen a sense of meaningfulness or understanding, and create a drive for urgency and action. Of course, many of us have potentially formative life experiences that fail to turn us into charismatic leaders. The ability to influence others in a transformational way accompanies many other factors, including competence, responsibility, vision, and circumstance.

The power of mystique should not be underestimated, however. As one can imagine, it must be difficult to build a sense of mystique when a leader is surrounded by the same people for many hours of every day. Indeed, at most ranks in an organization, competence, clarity, certainty, pragmatism, and teaching are much more valuable and productive skills. If anything, an up-and-coming leader does not create a sense of mystique in others around him or her so much as in those above. Supervisors, executives, and senior leaders, watching a highly competent, influential, and effective individual, might wonder, "How does this person do it?" and become intrigued. At the top ranks, the directionality of mystique is reversed: those who know the leader well may be less taken in by all aspects of the leader's strong personality, although they may remain suitably impressed with certain core aspects. For those below the senior leader, a sense of mystique, mystery, and intrigue can grow even more powerful with distance. Many who have never met or had any direct experience with a leader can feel that leader's mystique. It's a form of identification that comes primarily from within.

Mystique is the essence of charisma. We identify with leaders who are like us, exemplify qualities that we admire and desire but do not have, and ensnare or engage us with a sense of mystery or intrigue. But is there a net benefit to this charisma for organizations? I believe there can be. If the leader uses the charisma well, it can serve as an influence tactic—one more tool in the arsenal to create desired action. If the charisma is used for negative or poorly considered ends, then it is a powerful force that wastes energy on a pointless cause. Like any other tool, its value arises from its utility. Not all leaders have charisma, but some do. Not all leaders with charisma are effective and good, but some are very effective and very good. Under some circumstances, particularly moments of great trial or challenge, charismatic leadership can pull a group together and inspire focus like no other force.

Does this mean that organizations should look for leaders who have charisma or actively aim to develop charisma in emerging leaders? I don't think that charisma, like leadership, is always the answer. At some levels and under some circumstances, charisma is far less important than sheer competence. Organizations that parachute larger-than-life figures into their top leadership roles may get a short-term bang for the buck in terms of impact because of the mystique factor, but I doubt whether that mystique will stand up over time. Like credibility, mystique is easily lost and extremely difficult to regain. To deny that charisma exists and has power, however, is to put our heads in the sand about a fundamental social phenomenon. Not all leaders have it, but many of the great leaders do. It undeniably has a dark sense, yet it is something we seek out in those we wish to follow.

4

Secret 3

―――

REAL LEADERS DON'T PLAY POLITICS (THEY TAKE IT VERY SERIOUSLY)

My father, a wise, blue-collar, salt-of-the-earth man who earned every penny he ever made, said it best: "Watch out for that guy. He's a politician." To my father, a politician was the worst thing you could be. Straight shooters say what they mean and do what they say. They live by their word. They don't try to trick you, turn the tables on you, make promises they have no intention of keeping, say what they know you want to hear, cut you out of the loop, use you, or do an end run around you to reach their objectives. For my father, that was the one big turn-off of working for a large organization: way too much gamesmanship, politics, and backstabbing. Who needs it?

Most of us feel the same way. And yet we all know such people in our organizations. In fact, more often than not, politicians—meaning people who are skilled at getting what they want without necessarily having the authority or power to do so—seem to thrive in bureaucracies. They rise through the ranks and, as they do so, gain allies and supporters as well as recognition, reputation, and status. They also accumulate detractors and even enemies: people who feel used, pushed aside, outmaneuvered, and neglected. If those detractors aren't completely ousted, they always seem to be waiting in the wings, hoping for the politician to fail, ready to pounce if he or she does—and just as quick to jump back on the bandwagon when that "political bastard" favors them again. When an organization is dominated by politics, it's not pretty—an indication that trust is low, leadership is weak, and the organization is in distress.

As an executive coach, there have been many occasions when I've had to be the messenger of feedback in which a leader's colleagues, direct reports, and superiors describe him or her as being political. I know that stings. It's not a term that has any gloss or neutrality to it. It implies a disparagement of that person's character and an attack on the core of who he or she is, not just the way he or she behaves. One of my mentors, Joe Keilty, used to say that politicians kiss up and kick down: they tell the boss what the boss wants to hear; they look out for their own interests more than anyone else's; and they treat everyone around them badly. It's not easy to tell someone that he or she is a political slime ball, but occasionally this person needs to hear the news straight in order to change how he or she behaves and is perceived in the world.

As an executive coach and leadership expert, I don't see my role in life as being on a mission to eradicate politics and political behavior from the hallways, corner offices, and meeting rooms of corporate America. In fact, it is my belief, based on years of experience observing leaders and organizations, that politics is not a necessary evil in the leadership game; it is necessary. No leader achieves goals without politics. No organization is utopian because it is politics free. Instead, politics is the air leaders breathe and an important source of an organization's energy and dynamism. The fact that *politics* is such a dirty word only points to its status as another taboo of leadership. We don't like to acknowledge the existence of politics because we prefer an idealized and sanitized view of our leaders.

And yet if we ever encountered a leader who was truly not political, we would find that person disappointingly ineffective. Politics is a necessary skill for making leadership meaningful. When I work with leaders who have been labeled as too political by their colleagues, reports, and superiors, I don't coach them to change their ways in order to become better, more morally centered, and likable people; I teach them to change their ways because it's time, at this stage in their careers, to do the political thing differently. For a leader, appearing less political is a very political act. Like any other critical skill, it needs to be mastered.

ALL POLITICS IS BAD

Politics in the workplace differs from the politics we know from elections, but there are some similarities, too. Politicians who are competing in elections campaign for support for their issues and their own candidacy. They focus particularly on opinion leaders, those with sway over others, and try to garner as many votes as they can. They try to be well liked by everyone, kissing babies, and shaking hands because that sense of likeability can turn into passionate support. (FDR once said that every handshake is worth three hundred votes.) Workplace politicians do many of the same things, metaphorically. While we see electoral politics as full of staged rituals that are acceptable because they are traditional, we view any perceived lack of sincerity or any overt efforts to garner support in organizations as distasteful. Going after what you want by playing the game is somehow considered wrong.

I could cite many highly respected leadership and organizational experts for their negative views of politics. At the same time, I recognize that in the world of book reviews and jacket endorsements, this might be an impolitic thing for me to do. Oh, what the hell.

Henry Mintzberg, Bronfman Professor of Management at McGill University, is one of the smartest and most refreshingly unorthodox management and organizational experts in the world. Like Peter Drucker did, he recognizes the good and bad in our organizations. According to Mintzberg (1989, p. 236):

> I am no fan of politics in organizations. But neither am I a fan of illness. Yet I know we have to understand one like the other. In fact, politics can be viewed as a form of organizational illness, working both against and for the system. On one hand, politics can undermine healthy processes, infiltrating them to destroy them. But on the other, it can also work to strengthen a system, acting like fever to alert a system to a graver danger, even evoking the system's own protective and adaptive mechanisms.

In other words, Mintzberg (like most of us) believes that politics in organizations is a bad thing, but there's a good side: when we spot the existence of politics, we know something is terribly wrong. The patient is sick, and politics is the symptom. Recognizing that, we can rush the patient to the emergency ward and save his or her life.

Mintzberg thinks of politics in terms of gamesmanship too. He has even come up with names for those games, many of which you will read with a thrill of recognition: the insurgency game, the counterinsurgency game, the sponsorship game, the alliance-building game, the empire-building game, the budgeting game, the expertise game, the lording game, the line versus staff game, the rival camps game, the strategic candidates game, the whistle-blowing game, and the young Turks game.

From this perspective, politics indicates dissatisfaction within the ranks, conflict between power bases, and division between factions; it distracts people from important goals; and it uses up vital energy in unproductive pursuits. Mintzberg points out that some organizations are more prone to politics than others. Entrepreneurial organizations, for example, are not very political because the founder is a strong figure with a strong vision, and most people are focused on urgent objectives. The industrial (machine) organization is more prone to politics because it is more bureaucratic. Divisions have budgets that they scramble over. New generations can be in conflict with the generation in power. Line can be in conflict with management. Whistle-blowers might try to bring down the whole system. The professional organization is also prone to politics because hierarchy is flat and authority decentralized. In schools, law firms, and innovative start-ups, people assume power bases, alliances are formed, sponsorship is critical, and everyone needs to work gamely for whatever influence they can gain. In pure ideological organizations like cults, politics is not tolerated; because belief is so strong, people follow it without question.

All of this feels accurate, if viewed through a particular filter. Mintzberg does allow that politics can have a functional role. He thinks of it as a Darwinian process in which the strong survive, a conflict-heavy method by which various sides of an issue can be debated, a means by which change can be stimulated by dissatisfied people from within, and a way of easing the acceptance of executive decisions. Mintzberg implies that in a healthy organization, only a minimum of politics is necessary, but he also suggests that the existence of politics is a sign of life. Only a dead organization is free from politics because nobody cares what happens in it anymore. If politics is a necessity, Mintzberg believes, it is because disease goes with life. That said, we need to be vigilant about watching for it and try to lead lives that are as healthy as possible.

POLITICS AS A MODE OF POWER AND INFLUENCE

I disagree sharply with the view that politics is bad and should be eradicated from organizations, or at least minimized to whatever degree possible. Instead, I believe that politics is a tool that leaders must use to achieve their goals and, in the process, further the goals of their organization.

Leadership, in my definition, is an episodic process whereby an individual pursues his or her goals and vision by intentionally influencing others to perform various tasks to their full potential. Politics is an influence tactic that skillful leaders use to achieve their goals by getting others, regardless of rank, position, division, or formal affiliation, to perform on their behalf. Those others can include the CEO's executive assistant or the CEO, a direct report, a fellow vice president, or a team of consultants who are designing a new change agenda for the organization. The political leader knows how to stack the deck, play the right cards, build solid alliances, triangulate issues, and isolate those with conflicting points of view. The political leader does this in order to get what he or she wants: to achieve objectives and further his or her vision.

Mintzberg's discussion of organizational types and their propensity for politics is illuminating because it tells us how much the structure of an organization affects the way power and influence are used. Everyone knows that organizational charts don't tell the full story of how decisions are made in an organization. Title and rank do not always correspond to relative amounts of authority and influence, just as hierarchy is not a perfect map of power. This is because power comes in many different forms, all of them useful to getting things done.

According to Kathryn Stechart (1986), an expert on the differences in the way men and women use power, four distinct types of power are found in organizations: coercive, expert, referent, and perceived. Coercive power is about forcing people to do what you want. This can range from extortion and threat to simply having the authority to make others do what you want them to do because of position, status, and the ability to follow through on a perceived or implied threat. Coercive power can be highly effective in the short run, but it lasts only for as long as the threat exists and does not engender any loyalty or passion. Basically, it's impossible to influence someone to perform at his or her top potential through coercion for long.

Expert power is about the ability to demonstrate knowledge or proficiency such that others come to feel those skills are essential to the success of the organization. The person who has that knowledge or skill is given deference or authority because this power is useful and because there is a fear that he or she may withhold that power or bring it elsewhere. You can think of expert power as technical competence. Leaders tend to rise through the ranks because of their technical competence, despite our growing belief that hard skills are less important than soft skills. We value the individual's financial acumen, engineering knowledge, marketing savvy, or project management ability, for example, and continue to promote and reward this person for as long as his or her skills are beneficial.

Referent power is the power that a leader gains over someone who sees something of himself or herself in that leader. This homophily is all about perceived similarities. We are prone to follow someone who represents us in the most basic terms. If we share religious beliefs, ethnic backgrounds, nationalities, likes and dislikes, we are more likely to share or participate in a vision, which makes us more easily influenced to perform tasks in line with that vision.

Finally, Stechert talks about perceived power as being the most effective form of all. For example, we may believe that the CEO is the most technically knowledgeable person in the organization. We may also believe that the CEO is a lot like us, and we may even believe that the CEO has the most power to hurt us and force us to comply. Altogether, that's a considerable bandwidth of power. Charisma and magnetism are some means by which perceived power gets amplified. Basically, perceived power has some basis in reality, but the sense of power can be magnified dramatically through nonrational or emotional responses in followers.

Most decisions get made informally in organizations, in between the lines on the organizational chart, and are sanctioned or ratified only in the formal meetings between those who represent established power bases. It's rare that information flow, budgetary dollars, sponsorship and support, and all of the requisite activity and decision making follow in lockstep with the organizational chart. It's much more likely that a constant scramble is going on for all of these in an ever changing world. Politics, in that sense, is the dance of the shifting dynamics of power. It's about leveraging the power you have, in whatever circumstance you currently face, to achieve your goals.

THE COMPETITION
FOR FOLLOWERS

If power and influence are leadership commodities, then politics is the marketplace inside the organization through which
many deals and bargains are made. Everyone knows that leaders compete for resources; they grapple over slices of the
budget pie, CEO face time, and staff, for example. To a degree,
such resources are a way of quantifying power and influence.
Leaders also compete for followers with each other, with outside distractions, and with conflicting organizational priorities.

The ebb and flow of organizational energy is difficult to
harness, let alone use efficiently. Leaders can use positional or
hierarchical power to control resources, make moves, and define direction. But this power does not ensure that others will
follow, let alone perform up to their potential in service of
the leader's vision. Leaders are constantly vigilant in their
search for ways to win the competition for followers' hearts
and minds. This makes them, by definition, political. We
should not look at political behavior as necessarily good or
bad but neutral. To evaluate the extent to which political behavior is contributing to or distracting from the organization,
don't look to determine whether politics exists. Figure out
what it's being used to do.

BUT WHAT ABOUT
THE DARK SIDE?

In my view, political behavior is perceived as a negative at-
tribute of a leader when it does not reinforce a leader's vision
or the organization's needs. When colleagues, direct reports,

and supervisors point out that a leader is political, chances are that person is not using political skill with acumen.

Some people are ultrapolitical by nature. They walk into a room at a crowded party and immediately get a sense of who is powerful and who is not. Then they brush by those who aren't important to get at those who are. Eventually the behavior gets noticed and discussed, and a reputation develops. A consensus forms that such a person is not to be trusted and must be dealt with carefully.

Other people become political by experience. They learn the art of politics because they realize that being political is essential for achieving their objectives. Perhaps they have observed others getting what they want and wondered what those others have that they do not. Maybe they are immersed in a highly political environment and must learn to swim or sink. Or maybe they realize that position and authority don't influence people as much as one would hope and learn to play the game differently in order to be more effective. In any case, being political is just one more tool that leaders have.

Some leadership experts coach executives to be less political because they have a glossy, idealized, or politically correct view of what being a leader means. In reality, most organizations can't afford their leaders to mute or restrain those political skills. Efficiency, aggressiveness, and effectiveness would be sacrificed as a result. Instead, coaches need to recognize that leadership is a contact sport in which hands get dirty and noses are sometimes bloodied. It takes skill to be viewed as a leader who is not political while being politically astute. Despite what many may wish to think, leadership is a self-serving exercise that happens to benefit the organization as a whole. Political behavior that does not serve the leader's vision or the organization's direction is viewed negatively. Political behavior that does serve the leader's vision is called leadership.

In the movie *Power* (1986), Richard Gere plays an extremely successful political handler who has become tired of working for the highest bidder. Many of the well-financed politicians he helps get elected do not do any good once in office. To salve his conscience, he decides to select an honest candidate who stands for something and help that person get elected by using his dark arts. The candidate Gere selects is thrilled to receive his help and guidance. Gere tells the man how he must change his image and message in order to get elected, but the man refuses. He wouldn't have integrity if he did so. Gere argues that the candidate cannot accomplish any good if he does not succeed in getting elected. Put aside your integrity for the time being, he advises, and you can return to it once you are in power.

It often seems that the political leaders we elect are rarely able to live up to their potential or best intentions. Once they have sacrificed integrity to be elected, they must continue to sacrifice integrity to be reelected. Even a second-term president or a retiring senator is still beholden to the interest groups and powerful individuals who saw him or her elected in the first place. There is a fear that being political can be an effective way of gaining and maintaining power, but at significant cost. Does this mean we should avoid being political, or does it indicate that being political is a taboo—and a luxury that effective leaders can't afford?

Leaders who believe that they can stop being political once they reach the top are often deeply disappointed. In truth, being political will always be part of the game. Nevertheless, the skill set for being political changes as a leader rises in the ranks. A leader who is an up-and-coming middle manager will probably need to gain accolades and recognition from above, while creating supportive friends and allies all around and not distancing or turning off anyone in the process. A leader at the top of the organization might need to be viewed by followers as benevolent, compassionate, articulate, and visionary. But do those attributes have to be real, or is perception more important than the reality? The question reeks of being political. To many of the world's CEOs, the answer is self-evident: part of their job is to convince people of those perceptions, regardless of the truth. I doubt, however, that they would ever admit to that in public.

5

Secret 4

WOMEN MAKE BETTER LEADERS
(WHEN THAT'S WHAT THEY
REALLY WANT TO DO)

An outsider studying our culture from the headlines on business and news magazines might wonder what all the fuss is about. Women wanted the top jobs; then they got them; then they didn't want them anymore. Men wanted to keep women out; then they thought that becoming more feminine would give them a competitive advantage; then they got tough and ruthless all over again. Now women are nearly as ubiquitous as men in the middle management ranks, and there are enough women making an impact at the CEO level that no one can label them token representatives anymore. Male or female, boss or direct report, gender isn't supposed to matter in the corporate setting. But while things may look slightly better in terms of numbers, something is still not quite right below the surface. So how come the bulk of the research out there points to the same ugly problem? For instance, according to our research at LRI, women approaching top levels in organizations would overwhelmingly rather report to a man than another woman, and they would rather have men than women reporting to them as well.

Women are supposed to make better leaders, we've been told. So why don't other women want to follow them? Maybe those women know something that men are too afraid to discuss. To understand what that might be, let's think about the evolution of the women as leader in corporate America.

A BRIEF HISTORY
OF BRA BURNING

Almost forty years ago, women started burning bras and banging on the glass ceiling. Relegated to secretarial jobs and outposts like human resources, they were mad as hell and not going to take it anymore. A little bit of progress was made over the next decade or two, but the impediments to real inclusion were insidious and severe. Sometimes top executive floors didn't even have a women's restroom until a woman was named senior vice president; then the wrecking crews came in and knocked down a wall, put in a sink with a nice mirror, and tossed a few urinals into the dumpster. Not that it did much good. The old boys played golf and drank martinis and liked their women subservient; they weren't going to change in their hearts, no matter how much pressure got put on them to open structural, regulatory, and institutional doors. Those grumpy old men, and their sons and younger brothers and cousins and pals, thought women were too fragile, emotional, undisciplined, and frivolous to handle a serious executive position, let alone a C-level posting where ruthless, tough, ultracompetitive decisions needed to be made daily.

Women blew a gasket whenever they heard or perceived such bias. Fundamentally, they declared, *Women are the same as men!* They could be just as tough, just as ruthless, just as cold-hearted, calculated, and disciplined, and just as focused on making money and winning. They only needed men to change their perceptions and give women a legitimate shot. A generation of women who broke through the glass ceiling proceeded to live up to that claim. They talked like men and dressed like men. They held off on having children because it would interfere with their upward career trajectory. They didn't even dream of reaching down to lend a hand to young women on the way up. After all, that would identify them as women—members of a club they were trying to re-sign from, not join. Besides, no one had helped *them* on the way up. Women needed to be strong to survive in the Darwinian world of corporate America. They needed to be cruel to be kind.

For all their sacrifices, women still found bias, institutional resistance, and, worst of all, compensatory unfairness rampant in the executive ranks. "Equal pay for equal work" became the new rallying cry, and overall, there was progress. And indeed, little by little, men began to change. Working with women peers and working for women bosses began to affect male behavior, which in turn began to affect male thinking. They learned that sexist jokes, sexual harassment, asking for coffee, commenting on skirt length, holding open doors, picking up heavy boxes, and pretty much doing anything that defined or treated women differently from men was taboo. They could get written up, disciplined, and passed over for promotion. They could lose their job or get transferred to some outpost. They could get their company sued. As a result, men began to tread very, very carefully around women and let loose only once in a while, at the Christmas party or in the sanctity of the golf cart, so long as a powerful woman wasn't within hearing range. If the female director of national marketing strategy happened to be standing behind any guy who blew off a little steam about "women this" and "women that" or chortled over a sexist joke, the room would go so silent you could hear a pin drop.

Still, the rules were clear, and they made sense. Women were the new men. In time, they would learn to be just as bitter, mean, intolerant, demanding, and dismissive as men. So be it. Men still had their wives, daughters, and waitresses to lean on, if not push around.

But then came the 1990s, and men had to learn what to do and what not to do in the corporate setting all over again.

THE ROARING NINETIES

Sure, they can blame women. But maybe men brought it on themselves. After all, men were the ones whose urge to be cutthroat and ruthless tore the guts out of the organizational culture.

When reengineering became the rage in the 1980s and early 1990s, male leaders got busy. They culled whole layers out of their executive bureaucracy, laid off thousands of white-collar workers, got rid of silos, and flattened the organization with a steamroller. At the same time, information technology made communication, secretarial work, and data management as easy as typing. Throw in voice mail and e-mail, and not many needed secretaries. It was a new world of work.

Flattening the organization made one thing clear: without a hierarchy of bosses telling other bosses what their reports should do, people needed to think and talk in different ways. Suddenly they needed to get along better as teammates. They couldn't just order someone around anymore. They needed to get to know the person; care for, comfort, and anticipate his or her needs; and be more sensitive, more feminine.

At the same time, the economy started to roar, educated white-collar workers were suddenly in short supply, and women became a hot labor commodity. Women were recruited and promoted for their own sake, but they were also valued because they were genetically or socially engineered to be successful leaders in the new knowledge economy.

Ever since the industrial revolution, or at least the 1930s, the organization had been markedly masculine. The dominant mechanical school of organizational theory, for example, was founded on such ideas as centralized authority, specialization and expertise, division of labor, principles, rules, and regulations (Hackman and Porter, 1977). The emerging organization, however, was more feminine in gender because it was characterized by collaboration, the delegation of authority, empowerment, trust, openness, concern for the whole person, an emphasis on interpersonal relations, and the inevitability of interdependence.

Women, it would seem, were in the right place at the right time. If organizations were becoming more feminine and women were the undertapped labor resource in a booming economy, what could be wrong with that? Well, for one, it was confusing for men. By this point, men had been beaten up by women for thinking they were different. Now women began to think that way too. For years, the rule was that women were equal to men because they were the same as men; now they were equal to men but different. Women, it turned out, saw the world differently, worked differently with others, and reached their objectives differently; they even had different brains.

Back to boot camp for men. They'd learned to respond to women's needs before, and they could do it again. But there was an added twist to the problem: this time, men had to change.

SO SOFT IT'S HARD

Blame human resources. Men should have known better than to put women in charge.

With a flattened organizational structure and a knowledge economy that put a premium on such feminine characteristics as collaboration, trust, and sensitivity, it was only a matter of time before some social psychologist decided to start grooming men in a new way. If they were going to succeed in the organization as leaders, men needed to become a lot more like women. Men, being men, are willing to do whatever it takes to get ahead, so they bought into the idea and started doing team-building exercises, practicing how to hug and cry, and sharing their feelings in group therapy.

After all these years, men were now told that hard skills were not really that important when it came to leadership. Technical attributes were like tool belts; they could be picked up at the hardware store when needed and strapped on to suit the task at hand. You didn't need to be an engineer to run an oil company any more than you needed to be a chemist to run a drug company. The important capabilities were not the ones that could be found on your résumé; they were the ones that were so soft they were really hard. Men saw the world in black and white, but people, customers, markets, and complex problems were a rainbow of colors. Facts didn't matter as much as feelings. Being smart was way less important than being emotionally intelligent. This was in direct opposition to years of theory about how good decisions get made. Edward de Bono (1999) had counseled us that we need to parse issues and think about them rationally, emotionally, creatively, and in other ways in order to make clear decisions rather than let emotion suffuse thought.

Women, according to writers like Daniel Goleman (2005), had emotional intelligence in spades. All that time spent chatting instead of getting to the crux of important issues? That was really about bonding, openness, sharing, empathy, building rapport, and trust. How about the need to consult everyone in the organization from the boss to the janitor before making an important decision? That was all about consensus building, alignment, and seeing the issue from multiple perspectives.

During the boom years, it seemed to work. Productivity was high, stock prices rose, new markets emerged, and old markets got bigger and more profitable. Maybe this business of the organization becoming feminine wasn't so bad after all. Then the bubble burst, the economy contracted, and long-range projections for growth fell off a cliff. Time to batten down the hatches. After all, when the going gets tough, the tough get going.

That's when women started to cry.

WHO'S SORRY NOW?

When the going got tough, a lot of women decided they didn't want to be any tougher. Maybe all of that slaving for the big bucks, working yourself to the bone, and ripping the fabric of your family and personal life to shreds just wasn't worth it. Business and news magazines like *Fortune, FastCompany,* and the *New York Times Magazine* noted that "women aren't in the corner office" and "they don't want power, they're opting out." Warren Farrell's taboo-busting book, *Why Men Earn More* (2005), laid it out straight: women tend to put in less time than men, working fewer hours, and statistically, people who work forty-four hours a week make almost twice as much as those who work thirty-four hours. As a result, women still comprise fewer than 2 percent of Fortune 1000 CEOs and just 7.9 percent of Fortune 500 top earners. As Carol Hymowitz (2005) pointed out in an article in the *Wall Street Journal,* the reasons are many: women hit their prime child bearing years at the same time they are most pressured to prove themselves at work; they are reluctant to put in the 80-hour work week and globe trotting required for the corner office; they are too concentrated on staff positions like HR and marketing, where they never learn P&L responsibility; they don't have informed mentoring and networking opportunities, like golfing with the guys. These theories belie a consistent finding in the research: there is little difference between the leadership styles of successful male and female bosses. Hymowitz hit it right on the head when she stated, "The big problem is both sexes believe their own biased perceptions more than they believe [the facts]" (p. B1).

For all of these reasons and theories, research organizations like Catalyst claimed that women were leaving Fortune 500 companies at an astounding rate of fourteen hundred women per day. Where they were going was anyone's guess, but given the level of heated discussion over the issue of work–life balance, we can imagine that they were sick of the grind. Maybe power wasn't worth it. Maybe the glass ceiling was more like Plexiglas protection around a violent hockey game. Maybe women were not getting the intellectual stimulation they need, or, as a *New York Times* article pointed out, "they are just bored" (Deutsch, 2005). This possibility has prompted big companies like GE, Procter & Gamble, IBM, Booz Allen Hamilton, Ernst & Young, and Deloitte & Touche to put programs into place aimed at keeping women engaged.

Frankly, most men didn't have the luxury of wondering whether success was worth it; they were too busy scrambling to survive. If that's what a decade of forced caring amounted to—a parachute jump out of the corporate Lear Jet just because of a little turbulence—well, who needs you? No wonder a backlash has set in, in which real men/leaders like George W. Bush and Dick Cheney don't feel your pain, prefer to inflict pain on others, and never, ever say they're sorry.

And what's with all this crying stuff anyway? Few have talked about it. Few know how. Emotionality in the workplace has become acceptable, even encouraged, but isn't enough enough? Emotions are wonderful, powerful things. They can bolster a sense of mission, lend passion to an enterprise, bond teams together, and help clear the air, but they can also get in the way of what needs to be done and who needs to do it. Crying is an example. The women I know hate crying at work, but they just can't help themselves. When a discussion gets tense, whether about widget production or batting averages, men get animated, enthusiastic, passionate; women start to cry. They hate crying because it exposes their vulnerability, makes them feel like weaklings, and is embarrassing, but they can't stop. Furthermore, they hate it when other women cry too, just as much as the men do. As for men, crying completely disarms them. They don't know how to respond. They can't win; they can only lose.

So much for the soft side of leadership. Is that built-in emergency cry response whenever conflict surfaces why women prefer male bosses and male reports?

ON THE FOLLY OF REWARDING A, WHILE HOPING FOR B

The true nature of our problem, in my opinion, is explained best in Steve Kerr's famous essay, "On the Folly of Rewarding

A, While Hoping for B" (1975). Kerr described a common problem in human resource development initiatives. We say we want X, but we persist in rewarding Y. Consider the case of the feminization of leadership. A whole generation of leaders, men and women alike, were developed on the notion that sensitive, caring, coalition-building characteristics would lead to success. Open your arms, give your employees a big hug, explain everything they ever wanted to know about your motivations and underlying objectives, empower them, set them free, and they will perform for you at unprecedented levels, thereby securing your ultimate goals. It's a win–win–win situation.

Does it work like that in the real world? Well, as Ernest Hemingway once wrote, "Isn't it pretty to think so?"

In the real world, leadership is not always most effective when it is most caring, open, transparent, sensitive, and empowering. In fact, fear, manipulation, ruthlessness, power hoarding, and the competitive will to win at all costs are common characteristics of our best and most effective leaders. While that may not sound very warm and fuzzy, it cannot be ignored. So which is right? Is one approach better than the other? Perhaps the real answer is a fluid one without a clear-cut balance: a yin and yang between kiss and kick.

It sounds reasonable, but as Kerr points out, if we persist in viewing leadership in aspirational terms—as a host of noble behaviors we should strive for, not a collection of characteristics that actually means something—then we are going to miss the mark entirely. A whole generation of leaders will be taught one thing, while corporations will value, promote, and succeed based on an entirely different thing.

The organization may have become more feminine in structure and culture at the dawn of the knowledge era, but business results remain unabashedly male. Leadership may have softened in the past decade, but getting to the top, and staying there once you've made it, remains a tough, hard, ruthless, and overtly political act.

It isn't pretty to think so, but it's real.

IN THE FINAL ANALYSIS

Is leadership gender neutral, or does gender matter? Are men better at leadership in practice, or do women have better leadership attributes in theory?

I don't think we'll ever know. The important point, however, is that all leaders, prospective leaders, and followers—men and women alike—need to understand the true nature of leadership. It's messy rather than clear-cut. Some characteristics work in some situations. But to put our head in the sand and wish the ugly side away will cause us to fail.

It's unfortunate that gender and leadership is such a powerful taboo. Just ask Larry Summers. When the president of Harvard was asked to speculate in a debate about why women aren't better represented in the academic sciences, he suggested that gender differences, as observed in his two grandchildren, possibly play a role. As a controversial figure to begin with, Summers's public opinion on gender ultimately led to the loss of his job. And yet respected women scientists have speculated about the same ideas. Are we wired differently or raised differently? Who really knows?

I think that men and women could learn a lot from each other about leadership if they could talk about the elephant in the room. Women have all of the tools to be leaders. So do men. We all have different tools in different balances, and we all need to lean on some strengths over others or compensate for weaknesses. Do women really want to be leaders to the same degree as men? I don't know if there's a simple answer. Are they driven in the same way? Are they willing to pay the same price?

That's a question each leader, regardless of gender, has to ask himself or herself as the game is being played.

PART THREE

Taboos
of Position

Secret 5

THE DOUBLE STANDARD
IS FOR CAVEMEN
(AND THE CORNER OFFICE)

Harvey Golub, former CEO of American Express, used to smoke in his office. Golub was a great CEO, a powerful personality, a very effective leader, highly appreciated by his employees, shareholders, and competitors. So what made Golub's smoking habits problematic? Well, American Express is a smoke-free building. Was Golub aware of how negatively this abuse of privilege could have been perceived by others? In fact, he couldn't have cared less. He was a disproportionately important figure in the organization who happened to have a nicotine addiction. If feeding that addiction meant keeping his organization running well at the expense of some politically correct notion about double standards, then Golub was okay with that. In contrast, I recently heard a story about the executives of Wal-Mart. The company itself is notoriously frugal and concerned about the impact of costs on the bottom line. Despite their busy travel schedules, the executives who lead the largest corporation in the world stay at cheap hotels when traveling. To do otherwise would be to risk violating a value and creating the impression of a double standard.

Is there any issue more toxic in today's organizations than the notion of the double standard? It manifests itself most blatantly in terms of CEO pay, extravagant perks, and the kind of favoritism in which one set of standards is applied to top executives and another set to rank-and-file employees. When the economy is good, we tend to overlook such differentiation, comforted perhaps by the idea that a rising tide raises all boats. When the cycle turns, however, the resentment of unfair treatment brings a scrutiny of the double standard akin to a modern witch hunt.

The taboo is simple: leaders should avoid any impression that they are the beneficiaries of special treatment. Our politicians are the most public demonstrators of this sensibility. Consider the 2004 presidential election between John Kerry and George W. Bush. Both men came from privileged backgrounds—one merely very well-to-do, the other extremely wealthy. Both attended elite schools at every level of education, and received special treatment throughout their public and private careers by those who saw their tremendous potential. And yet both also attempted to outdo one another in conveying an impression of being ordinary folk in touch with ordinary Americans. John Kerry's political commercials focused on his humble beginnings and service to the American people, overlooking his marriage to a woman in command of a $1 billion fortune. George W. Bush's persona is a masterful display of common touch, and his speaking style demonstrates a bemused antielitism that many voters found comforting and refreshing.

Notice too that our business leaders, when writing their biographies or answering questions in interviews, tend to emphasize humble origins and everyday passions over anything that might strike people as being refined, privileged, or rarefied. We prefer to think of an elite business leader as the child of a mill worker or the child of the public school system, blessed by the fortunes of this great country. We prefer not to hear about the young man so obsessed with personal ambition that he worked hard enough to make it into an Ivy League school and gained access to elite connections that gave him a necessary foothold for later accomplishments.

The message leaders would like to convey through this reticence is that they are not recipients of special treatment and are, in fact, no different from the rest of us. At some level, they sense that the public's attitude to the double standard is deeply negative. And yet, as with all other taboos, a complicated set of emotions is involved. As much as it likes to deplore double standards, the public is also fascinated by them. Consider our obsession with Hollywood stars and members of royalty. Not surprisingly, leaders also feel one way about double standards in private and another way on the record. In the gap between those two extremes exists the electric nerve of the taboo.

THE TRAPPINGS OF POWER

CEO pay is the most egregious example of any perceived double standards in today's business world. The sheer numbers are staggering. Ten million dollars in salary, $20 million in bonuses, $100 million or so in stock options. *How can one person in an organization be worth that much money? Why would anyone even want that much? What could this person possibly spend it on?* When you throw in the perks and payoffs that go with the dollars, the sense of disproportion becomes surreal. It's not just the money. Other perks can include a private Lear

jet, a \$5 million pied-à-terre, a dozen country club member-
ships, a two-hundred-acre summer home by the sea, laundry
service, music lessons, and pet grooming. Even more damag-
ing, the information about such trappings of power seems to
be released when the executive is under pressure over poor
company performance. This confirms a general impression
that Nero has been fiddling while Rome burns.

We are both shocked and titillated by each new revela-
tion. Several very public CEOs could be described as poster
children for overdoing it. Dick Grasso, head of the New York
Stock Exchange (NYSE), is one of them. Grasso was a true
success story in the American mode. He started at the NYSE
at an entry-level position, working in the proverbial mailroom, and climbed the ranks over the next thirty years until
he reached the top position. From that leadership post, he
oversaw the NYSE's evolution through a period of tremendous technological change; he maintained public confidence
in the capitalist shareholder system despite a wave of corporate accounting scandals and a sense of entrenched favoritism
in the financial companies that create stock offerings; and he
helped the organization literally survive the devastating terrorist attacks on the World Trade Center in September 2001.
For all of these accomplishments and more, he was rewarded
handsomely. When the extent of those rewards was revealed,
he fell with a mighty thud.

The double-standard taboo that got exposed in Grasso's
case was all the more electrifying because the NYSE is a
nonprofit organization. Although no one could ever imagine
the beating heart of Wall Street functioning or even thinking
like a nonprofit in any ordinary sense, nevertheless, that word
nonprofit was repeated over and over in news reports discussing the "scandal." It was as though Grasso, as leader of
some charity like the United Way, had cooked the books and

robbed donors blind at the expense of malnourished children in the Third World.

The truth was somewhat different. Grasso's compensation package was awarded to him by his board of directors. Certainly most of those board members had been appointed because of their support for and friendship with Grasso, but they also had impeccable credentials as leaders of the very institutions that Grasso was being paid to serve. To suggest that Grasso was caught with his hand in the cookie jar is a complete mischaracterization of what happened. Indeed, Grasso was operating completely within the boundaries of the rules by which he had played his entire life. Publicly, however, Grasso had broken a taboo.

Jack Welch, former CEO of GE, encountered a different aspect of the double-standard taboo. Many would argue that Welch was the greatest CEO of the twentieth century. While he was overseeing GE's phenomenal growth, no one complained about his compensation or called any aspect of it into question. During his messy divorce, however, details of his retirement package became public knowledge. In addition to a great deal more money than had been known about, Welch was also the beneficiary of a multimillion-dollar Manhattan apartment and use of the corporate jet, among other surprises. Most shocking of all, Welch, an extremely wealthy man, had his dry cleaning services covered too.

To those already frothing about the excesses of double standards, this information was proof that even Saint Jack was corrupt. Why in Thomas Edison's name should GE shareholders pay for Welch's dry cleaning when he no longer ran the company? In fact, Welch's benefits were not out of line with what other CEOs have typically received. More significant still, few of those other CEOs have ever come close to producing the value that Welch created for shareholders.

Indeed, the benefits of his leadership extended beyond GE, raising the bar for executive performance at companies everywhere. And yet there was something about the idea of Jack Welch getting his dry cleaning expenses reimbursed that upset people. Welch unwittingly had broken a taboo, and his luster was a touch less shiny as a result.

FROM THE CEO'S POINT OF VIEW

Why are executives surprised by negative reactions to their own double standards? Because the double standard is very standard to them.

CEOs are treated differently in many different ways. Unlike ordinary mortals, they do not wait in line or worry about petty rules that ordinary employees must strictly adhere to. When budgets are tight, don't expect the CEO to fly coach even though everyone else must. In a nonsmoking office, don't be surprised to see the CEO enjoying a cigar during a meeting.

The people who run large companies today make millions of dollars and receive special treatment, but so do others in our society. Julia Roberts, the film actress, has said publicly that she thinks it is ludicrous that she is paid $20 million to star in a Hollywood movie. But she has also noted that the movies in which she is the star gross hundreds of millions of dollars, employ thousands of workers, and generate revenue for large, powerful companies. Why shouldn't she be a primary benefactor of that wealth generation? In addition, she is beset by the never-ceasing glare of media attention and has virtually no private life within the public realm. Is it any wonder that she expects door-to-door limousine service, a personal trainer to meet her at her hotel every morning, and friends, hangers-on, and employees to take care of her smallest needs? For every Julia Roberts who succeeds, there are thousands of actresses whose efforts fall short. It's an equation that should mean something in determining value. Indeed, we reward our star professional athletes in much the same way, rarely, if ever, decrying their special treatment. Tiger Woods makes $80 million a year in endorsements, whether he picks up a golf club or not. We don't think that he should give back big bonuses or stop riding in private jets just because he doesn't win back-to-back majors one season. We think it's perfectly reasonable given the extent of everything he has accomplished in his career thus far.

Still, this nonjudgmental attitude does not seem to apply to business leaders, perhaps because we view them less as stars than as employees. Or maybe it is because we expect more from them in terms of leadership. However, in a very real sense, those CEOs and top executives are much like Julia Roberts or Tiger Woods. As talented experts in a specialized field, they create value that far exceeds the salaries they earn.

The truth is that CEOs feel perfectly justified in receiving salaries, bonuses, and special favors that seem outrageous to the rest of us. From their perspective, they are increasing shareholder value, running a complex operation, putting future generations in a better position to thrive, making many people around them rich, launching great products, and having a profound impact on the world. Few executives would ever go on the record and say so, but in private, most would dismiss any questions about their extravagant treatment. The justifications they provide might fall into one of three categories:

- *The public doesn't have all the information.* The public
  sees some raw numbers, including the CEO's salary
  and the company's stock performance, but has no
  idea about the company's real value or how much
  the CEO has contributed to that value historically
  or what the CEO has done to prepare for a successful future long after his or her departure. The public
  also has no idea how hard the CEO has worked to
  achieve his or her expertise or experience in the
  first place or what personal and career sacrifices he
  or she has made along the way. Finally, the public
  doesn't understand the extent to which the CEO
  is on call and in service to the organization all the
  time. If perks and benefits extend into the CEO's
  private life, chances are that the CEO has no private
  life. The country club membership, the second home,
  the Lear jet, the laundry and catering expenses:
  all are provided to the CEO because they are
  connected to his or her service of the company.
  Nothing is personal; it's all business. A CEO's job
  is not like that of an employee at any other level.
  It has no physical, emotional, or mental boundaries.

- *It's a free market.* The amount a CEO receives in
  salary is not pulled out of thin air. Rather, it is a
  rational number tied to the CEO's perceived value
  and based on what the market will bear. No one
  criticizes Tiger Woods for getting $40 million to
  wear Nike's swoosh and $5 million to appear in
  American Express ads. We assume that those organizations are making a rational decision based on
  their perception of Woods's value to their brand, and
  paying him accordingly, beating out competitors in

the process. No one questions whether Hollywood studios are throwing their money away when they sign Julia Roberts to open their next blockbuster picture. In the same way, publicly held companies are not going to reward a CEO beyond his or her market value. A CEO's salary is not a sign of boundless gluttony; it is a barometer of market conditions.

- *Keeping score: The drive to win.* CEOs themselves may be guilty of using perks, benefits, and bonuses in another way. They are very competitive people by nature; they know what their colleagues in other organizations are getting, and they like to keep score. Salary and bonuses is one form of score keeping. Flipping to the newspaper article about executive compensation, a CEO is just as likely to look at the numbers as the rest of us, but he or she is probably comparing his or her own salary with a colleague's. If the numbers are out of whack, the CEO is bound to feel competitive juices flowing. It may seem strange or petty to those who do not feel such urges, but it is part of the excitement of the game and critical to the drive to win. Consider the ongoing naval arms race among high-tech CEOs. Fifteen years ago Larry Ellison, CEO of Oracle, bought a yacht for $12 million. Jim Clark, founder of Silicon Graphics, wanted a bigger boat that was going to cost him $30 million, so he hurried the Netscape initial public offering and inadvertently began the high-tech bubble. Ellison countered again with an $80 million yacht. Paul Allen, cofounder of Microsoft, not to be outdone, bought his yacht for $100 million. Meanwhile,

Clark is at it once more, building a schooner that's estimated to cost $100 million too. If you think that these men don't know the exact size, cost, and other details of their boats, you don't know how a CEO's mind works.

RECALIBRATING THE DOUBLE STANDARD

In our egalitarian society, few of us like to acknowledge that double standards exist. As a hot button issue, the idea brings up strong and immediate impressions of social injustice and special treatment: tax breaks for the rich, military deferments for the well connected, legacy appointments to elite colleges for the children of the wealthy, affirmative action or racial profiling for minorities. We'd prefer to believe that the existence of various forms of the double standard is either an anomaly of privilege or temporary bandages for righting old wrongs.

And yet there are complex aspects to any argument that some people should or should not get more than others. In addition to living in an egalitarian society, we live in a capitalist one. We believe that people should be rewarded differently depending on the market value of the work they do, the services they provide, or the assets they possess. By default, this means that some people will have more, get more, and be able to do more than others.

We also believe in the American dream—the idea that we have an inalienable right to build a prosperous life for ourselves and pass on that prosperity and security to our children. Under such a system, is it possible or even rational to imagine each generation beginning its own journey from the same starting point?

As a society, we believe that some people are more talented than others, and we applaud those capabilities and accomplishments. In our obsession with fame and uniqueness, we shine a bright light on such people, on and off the job, and treat them like royalty. Whose fault is it that teachers and nurses don't get celebrated and rewarded like pop stars and second basemen? It's our fault. We don't value those capabilities or services as much as we say that we should.

To an objective observer, the answer is clear. We make the decision to differentiate with the double standard every day. Should we be concerned at how large or shocking the gap between the elite few and the many becomes? It doesn't make any rational sense, and yet the taboo remains. Is our reaction to the double standard an outmoded concern that should wither and disappear? Or is it a healthy way to keep in check the avarice and elitism inherent in our social system? Taboos can be rooted in superstition. They can also be functional, providing a necessary barrier to bad habits.

Is there any reason to believe that the taboo of the double standard has a negative or positive impact on our business leaders? On the one hand, we need to compensate and support our business leaders adequately because their talent is so rare and their value so critical. On the other hand, human beings can be extremely sensitive to feelings of justice, fairness, and equity. Peter Drucker and other theorists warned that in a healthy organization, executive pay should not exceed that of average worker by more than four times. Yet upward mobility is so much more available to all people today. Perhaps the double standard provides a healthy incentive for entrepreneurial energy.

When it comes to special treatment in an organization, should it bother us that some people receive exceptions to the general rule? The treatment can be justified in terms of relative contributions. But what are the costs? Does the erosion of consistency carry with it a more significant burden than we may realize? Credibility is an important currency for leaders. One of our most powerful definitions of credibility can be summed up in the following way: a leader does what he or she says he or she will do. In other words, this person walks the talk. If a leader proclaims that we must all tighten our belts to survive a rough period and then continues to receive lavish treatment; or if a leader freezes bonuses but garners them himself or herself; or if a leader transgresses on a core value that he or she has declared sacrosanct, isn't this person's credibility greatly diminished in the eyes of followers? On a personal level, a danger exists that special treatment can blind or protect a CEO from unwelcome but ultimately helpful data. Many times I have been called in by a CEO to conduct extensive evaluations of that CEO's top people, but been told by the CEO that he or she doesn't need that kind of assessment. Is the CEO the best judge of that fact? Who is going to contradict the CEO in an environment in which the double standard is the norm?

The debate remains open, and the answers are murky and situational. The question for future leaders should be: Are you comfortable with the costs and benefits of operating under a double standard? The question for companies should be: Is your organization healthier without the double standard, or is it being put at a competitive disadvantage because of that aversion?

7

Secret 6

THOU SHALT NOT PLAY FAVORITES WITH FRIENDS AND FAMILY (EXCEPT WHEN IT MAKES A LOT OF SENSE)

Do leaders really care about merit? Should the most talented person always get the job, or is it better that key positions be held by friends and allies? Is it more important for a leader to be surrounded with the best people or with people he or she feels comfortable with and can trust?

One of the touchiest issues in corporate politics today is the role of favoritism. In a publicly traded company where thousands of people work, is it right that anyone should get ahead simply because he or she is related to the boss, has worked closely with this leader before, or knows him or her well socially? For those who don't share DNA or country club membership with the leader, these relationships can lead to a familiar emotion. It's the kind of feeling that we experienced in grade school when we weren't chosen by the cool kids, or in college when we stood patiently in the rope line at some popular nightclub while the doorman mysteriously chose to let others slide through.

Theoretically, in a capitalist system, we believe that the marketplace, not genealogy, should determine who gets the opportunities and succeeds. American society, with its founding myth as a home for immigrants, self-starters, and high achievers, is predicated on the idea that getting ahead is all about effort, determination, and success, not heredity. But we also believe in the value of connections. Any parent who has worked hard understands the lure of wanting to pass on some help to his or her children. It's only natural. Indeed, there's a sense of warranted privilege behind the idea that our children deserve to be able to take advantage of the status, lifestyle, or opportunities that we have obtained. Nevertheless, although this sentiment gets a wink and a nudge in such traditions of status as legacy acceptances at college, it's different in the corporate world. Despite the fact that many great companies were built by families over several generations, there's still a whiff of a bad smell that can be detected whenever the CEO promotes his or her son or daughter to the head of a division. Critics are bound to think that the no-good, spoiled layabout got there by ordainment, not by hard work. They may even be right.

But does this really matter in the end? Is there any merit behind the leader's practice of promoting friends and family? If so, do the pluses outweigh the minuses? If not, why do so many leaders engage in such practices? Certainly, promoting friends and family is not just a holdover habit of another age; it's one tradition that continues to thrive regardless of the pressures for change.

It's a taboo to promote friends and family, but leaders do it anyway. It's also a taboo for people to treat the boss's powerful friend or family member differently, but those who don't probably have the Darwinian instincts of a dodo bird. In fact, the entire issue puts everyone involved into a double or triple bind and may even hamper the effectiveness of the organization as a result.

So why doesn't anyone ever talk openly about the fact that favoritism and even nepotism are rife in corporations and determine the best course of action accordingly?

Oh, right, I forgot. It's a taboo.

WHY DOES THE LEADER DO IT?

Rupert Murdoch, the chairman and CEO of Newscorp, is a titan. That's the term that people use very loosely when they describe people who head media companies, but doesn't Murdoch seem as though he would be a titan no matter what he did? I can picture Murdoch coaching Little League, working as a janitor, or participating in a knitting class, and I still think he'd come across as a titan. The man has a ruthless, tough, incredibly aggressive, and success-driven persona that seems like a force of nature akin to a hurricane or volcano eruption. He created one of the largest and most successful media conglomerates in the world, rules it like Augustus once ran the Roman Empire, and maintains an iron grip on power despite the fact that he is at an age when most CEOs are playing shuffleboard.

Nearly every move Murdoch has ever made has paid off by making his organization more powerful and his shareholders wealthier. Can you imagine working for Murdoch or even standing up in a shareholder meeting and questioning him over putting his children into highly visible and senior positions within the organization? His glare alone would probably vaporize you on the spot. And yet who didn't feel a slight kernel of doubt when Murdoch anointed his thirty-year-old son, Lachlan, as the head of Star Europe and his heir apparent? There was something oddly anachronistic, robber-baronish, and even Enron-esque to the practice of treating a global company like a private fiefdom. Indeed, the royal family quality of the saga was reinforced when Lachlan mysteriously resigned.

So why do the Rupert Murdochs of the world and the many corporate leaders we rarely hear about, like Ned Johnson at Fidelity and Brian Roberts at Comcast, lose so little sleep over how such behavior gets perceived by the rest of us? For a simple reason: they don't see it the same way. Much of the motivation and rationale for favoritism and nepotism can be uncovered by considering the real nature of leadership. Leaders are people too. Their emotions and perspectives shape and influence their decisions in ways that we don't always get at first glance. For example, few of us appreciate how lonely it can be at the top. It may sound like a cliché, but in it lies a grain of truth. A leader's life is consumed by his or her role, with very little time set aside for extracurricular activities. What might be extracurricular to us is work related to the leader: the fishing trip, the golf game, the dinner party, the African safari. Try separating leaders from their thought processes, pending decisions, and thirst for relevant ideas and information even for a minute. It just doesn't happen. Is it any surprise, then, that they view their work as an extension of personal life? The line is blurry, if it even exists. Why should it matter to anyone if people the leader knows from the social realm slide into the work realm? For the leader, it's virtually the same universe. In other words, a leader is simply not hung up on the idea of separating friends and family from the job, despite the opinions of the chattering class.

This is not to say that leaders choose people for their inner circle who have no reason to be there. To leaders, those reasons are sound, and they relate to trust, certainty, and predictability. It seems ironic, and it may not be macho to admit, but the powerful people who run organizations are actually in positions of extreme vulnerability. So much depends on them, and yet they are also completely dependent on others. It matters to whom they turn for advice, confidential conversation, strategic thinking, information, opinion, perspective, and emotional support. Why would any leader question the value of having trusted lieutenants in place around him or her? It's only natural that leaders often find such trusted lieutenants by turning to the family, social, or work environments that they know so well.

Moreover, knowing someone and feeling comfortable with that person is not the primary reason the leader has chosen him or her. What matters to the leader is knowing how that person thinks, what skills and capabilities he or she brings to the job, and how reliably he or she performs. The leader knows that his or her best friend and a former colleague has a flawless sense of timing when it comes to marketing new products. So he or she brings that friend over to become the new head of marketing as the company is gearing up for its next major product launch. Others, not privy to this experience, may question that decision because they don't have the same data the leader possesses. To the leader, it's about certainty and predictability. He or she has worked with that friend before, knows that friend's character and strengths and weaknesses, is comfortable with the friend, and has personally experienced how well that friend delivers in a difficult situation. More than anything else, leaders hate surprises. Once they've made a decision, they want to check it off the list and move on, certain that it will be accomplished. They don't want the anxiety of wondering whether this person will come through.

But there's more to the taboo of favoritism than just trust and reliability. Would it surprise you if politics also entered the equation? Politics at senior levels can be brutal. Trusted friends and family members make important political allies. They are inclined to watch the leader's back and support him or her at critical moments because of the depth of their relationship. They may also owe the leader a great deal, and the leader may be more than willing to draw interest on those debts whenever necessary. On a board of directors, for example, why wouldn't the chair and CEO want the board stacked with as many allies as possible? CEOs want their decisions to go their way. They want a supportive board, not one that is waiting for their first bad move. They want to know that they can walk into the room and discuss challenges relatively openly rather than always being wary. If the board of directors owes the leader for various reasons, so much the better. Leadership, after all, has a transactional component to it. It is the process by which a leader accomplishes objectives.

Finally, there's a third, and somewhat more selfish (if still understandable), motivation for loading up on friends and family. Leaders, never lacking in ego, think they probably ought to live forever. Short of being able to clone yourself, one form of immortality comes from seeing your own likeness in front of you. The leaders I have worked with who have been succeeded by people they have mentored closely are enormously proud of that accomplishment. To a degree, they see that individual as an extension of themselves. Gail Sheehy, in her book *New Passages* (1995), calls it "generativity." Leaders who see their children take over are similarly moved. There's a sense that the organization, which the leader has worked so hard to build, will be even more of a legacy if it is in the hands of one's children. There's also a feeling of well-earned privilege in that transfer of power. It took a lot to get as far as the leader has gotten. He or she earned it and should be able to take advantage of that effort by passing the keys to the next generation. It may not be a selfless emotion or a particularly sound one, but it's a real emotion, one that influences some of the most critical decisions the leader ever makes.

IT ALL MAKES SENSE, EXCEPT FOR A FEW PROBLEMS

Do leaders really know what they are getting when they select a friend or family member for a key role? It is said that love is blind; well, so is favoritism. It can be very difficult for leaders to form an objective and well-rounded assessment of someone they know well. They may know aspects of that person's character and behavior and understand how that person functions under certain circumstances, but they may not know everything. This is not unusual for any relationship, close or distant. The problem when it comes to favoritism, however, is the difficult position others are put into as a result.

Right or wrong, a perception exists that a favorite will always get the benefit of the doubt, and at the expense of others. The fact that the favorite has the leader's ear creates a huge fluctuation in the power dynamic. When an anointed favorite screws up, others are less likely to call that person on mistakes. When something goes wrong in the business, others tread lightly around that person. Unbeknown to the leader, the favorite may even play up, exaggerate, or use the perception of power arising from that special relationship against others in the organization. In fact, the leader may be the last one to know that such a dynamic exists.

I encountered some of these problems when I coached a CEO on how to fire a close friend. In this case, the friend was a poor cultural fit for the leader's organization. In a frugal work culture, the friend always flew first class, stayed in the best suites, and enjoyed his expense account with gusto. In a highly collegial and cooperative executive team, the friend was extremely political. He dropped overt hints about his special relationship with the CEO whenever he needed to win an argument or a position. To the CEO, these gruff, irascible, and contrarian personality traits were part of the friend's charm. Moreover, the friend had strong technical skills of great value to the organization. Nevertheless, that friend was a toxic presence on the executive team.

It was difficult for the CEO to see this, and it was difficult for others to approach the CEO with the information. During the period in which nothing was said and nothing was done, the CEO lost credibility with his team. Trust and morale suffered as a result, and the CEO's decisions began to be looked on with doubt, and even cynicism. Finally, a more senior member of the executive team took personal risk to his career to tell the CEO what was really going on. The CEO was shocked, but he was a solid leader with a great sense of responsibility and accountability. He responded not by punishing the whistle-blower or bitterly denying the truth, but by dealing with the situation. After assessing the facts, he determined that it was necessary to let his friend go, despite that friend's superb managerial capabilities.

This may constitute a kind of worst-case scenario, but favoritism brings with it subtle dangers. One of those dangers has to do with perspective. Every leader must deal with the problem of how to obtain accurate information in a timely manner. A leader might hope that having trusted friends and allies around provides a way of obtaining good data, but the opposite can be the case. When leaders surround themselves with friends and family, a bubble effect can result. They may withhold or even block contrary points of view. Or, more insidious, the decreased diversity of perspectives may narrow the data field to such a degree that the leader never even knows that contrary facts exist. You can imagine how the members of an old boy's network don't always recognize what life is like on the other side of the fence. In today's global economy, it is vital to understand how others see the world, because important personnel and customer decisions rest on that knowledge. A leader who has a fondness for bringing in old college buddies may find himself or herself with a limited view of what's going on in the world, what's going to happen next, and what's possible.

It's very difficult for anyone to tell leaders what they don't necessarily want to hear. In an organization rife with favoritism, it can be doubly hard for anyone outside that inner circle to approach a leader with critical information or feedback.

SHOULD THE LEADER
DO ANYTHING DIFFERENT?

Where do the chips fall? Given the pluses and the minuses, is it right for leaders to surround themselves with favorites?

Who cares? It's an irrelevant question. Leaders are going to do what they deem necessary to feel comfortable, protected, supported, and powerful. Whenever this question has come up in my own dealings with leaders, I answer: "You're right that you're going to have favorites. It's part of your nature, it's socially understandable, and it's the real world. The human element of who you are as a leader is going to influence how you run a company."

Leaders can protect themselves from negative charges of favoritism, however. If favorites are in place for reasons of trust, capability, and security, perhaps the leader can also make the rules of access and conduct transparent and clear. A culture of deep personal relationships at the executive level has often been conducive to great organizational success. Strong leaders surround themselves with favorites because they move fast, work hard, and are ferociously focused on winning. Favorites, by definition, are people whom leaders think will help in that regard. It shouldn't be a taboo to have favorites, and it shouldn't be a taboo to talk about the issues that arise as a result. It's going to happen, regardless of what may seem politically correct. We may as well bring the issue out of the dark and expose it to the light.

8

Secret 7

A LEADER'S FUNDAMENTAL DUTY IS TO GROOM A SUCCESSOR (BUT IT HURTS LIKE HELL)

In terms of leadership succession, consider how far we've come since Louis XIV.

Ascending to the monarchy of France at the age of thirteen, the Sun King, as he became known, ruled for the next seventy-two years. Over that incredible stretch of time, it should surprise no one that Louis became increasingly autocratic and dictatorial. Little by little, he integrated himself into the operations of government until he oversaw every aspect of his administration. No detail was too large or too small for his attention. Louis even gave military advice to his generals, accompanying the army on the ground whenever it made another foray into a foreign country to try to expand his empire. The generals flattered Louis as a military genius, of course, then did everything in their power to try to rectify his mistakes, compensate for his ignorance, and somehow still achieve the objectives he sought.

Naturally Louis thought he was indispensable to the running of his country and irreplaceable at its helm. He even coined a phrase that characterized his perspective on the matter: "L'état, c'est moi." For those of you whose French is a little rusty, here's a translation: "The state, it's me." And after seventy-two years, who could argue with him?

Louis was called the Sun King because he thought of himself as a modern Apollo, the god of light who provided patronage over the arts. But the moniker could just as easily have been referring to the sun at the center of the galaxy. After all, Louis didn't just inhabit the world like the rest of us; the world revolved around him. Not for him, any of that nonsense about empowering people and building up the skills and experiences of worthy successors. Indeed, the degree to which he centralized control of government and bankrupted the country through wars and building great palaces (including the beautiful, extravagant, and costly Versailles) sowed the seeds of the French Revolution.

Plenty of kings, pharaohs, tyrants, and cult leaders have acted the same way throughout history. Fortunately, the enlightened leadership of today's organizations has gotten over any sense of entitlement, divine right, and infallibility. CEOs and top executives understand that leadership is not a lifetime appointment, and no single individual, even the founder, is more important than the organization as a whole. Instead, every leader holds his or her position in trust, as a steward of the organization, whose obligation is to gently and effectively pass on the reins to the next generation. Some leaders have even declared, publicly and frequently, that the most important task they have is to find a worthy successor.

Yeah, sure. If all that is true, how come leaders hate thinking about succession so much? How come they almost always overstay their welcome, undercut or sabotage their successors, and probably cheer in secret when they fail and cry when they succeed? How come they have to be dragged kicking and screaming from their corner offices, fingernails clawing and scratching to hold onto their desks until the bitter end?

Maybe the thought of deliberately picking the person who will sit in your chair, wear your clothes, sleep with your spouse, and kiss your children on the forehead before bedtime every night once you are buried in the ground is a little less pleasant than it sounds. In fact, metaphorically or otherwise, it's a taboo.

EMPOWERMENT IS BEST WHEN FLYING SOLO

As the saying goes, if you're doing the work of two or more people, chances are you're a manager. This isn't a comment on the quality or capability of the average worker. Instead, it's a comment on the nature of being in charge. Assuming the duties of a manager requires an innate desire to put yourself forward, above others, as the person able to get stuff done and make things happen. For most managers, this comes so naturally that it's hard to let go of the constant thought: "I'm better at this. No one else can really get it done. Without me, this place would fall apart in a New York minute."

Sure, now that you're manager, you're supposed to guide and direct the efforts of those around you, but who's kidding who? No one else really cares whether this stuff gets done. No one else has the same sense of responsibility, duty, and obligation. No one else sees the big picture and the nagging details that color it in.

Still, there comes a time when the amount of work is physically impossible for one person to supervise directly. Being a manager at that level starts to require a different skill set. If you can't watch an employee's every move and guide his or her hand with yours, you need to learn a complicated new game. The game requires pretending to trust that people can function on their own when you are not there to watch, while also having the ability to motivate, inspire, threaten, and manipulate them to want to do the job as much as you want them to do it.

In a lot of business books, this is a good description of the act of leadership. The ceding of responsibility and capability to someone below you is called empowerment.

In reality, leaders are comfortable empowering themselves, but they tend to have a lot more difficulty empowering others. First, leaders amass power as a driver. They see power as a tool for accomplishing what they set out to do and believe innately that the more power they have, the more they will be able to get done. Empowerment, by definition, means giving up some power, and leaders just aren't very good at doing that, even if it will help them achieve the goals that they've amassed power to accomplish. If that sounds like a catch-22, it should. It's also one of those uncomfortable, messy, difficult-to-rationalize facts of life that go hand in hand with why anyone would have the urge to lead in the first place.

Second, not every direct report in an organization is empowerment receptive, despite what current leadership theory might claim. Acting independently in an effective way requires the right combination of skill and will. Assuming that everyone has the same amount of skill and will is nonsense, and yet that is the politically correct thing to do, and it pervades our society. We look at a roomful of school children and refuse to rank them on ability; instead, we give out ribbons and applause for participation. We ignore their will to win and pretend that they are great even when they don't rise to the occasion. On the playground, however, the kid with

the most skill and will is easy to identify. This child is winning the game, getting the attention, and dominating others
with his or her view of how things should be done. Provide
that kid with empowerment, and watch out; you'll soon find
that he or she is no longer easy to control. In truth, this is
what happens to leaders too.

In fact, empowering the people who are empowerment
receptive is almost a waste of time. Chances are that they've
instinctively grabbed all the power they can from the moment they started sensing its existence. Giving them more
power starts to feel like giving bullets to someone who is out
to get you. For a leader who believes that power is important,
giving power away simply stops making sense when the
person already knows what to do with it. I'm reminded of
the executive I coached who wanted to get more out of a key
report. Watching them in action, I saw how much the report
held back in meetings, kept thoughts to himself, and generally went along with whatever the executive wanted. The
executive coaxed this person not to be afraid of speaking up
and contradicting him in meetings because that was the kind
of leadership he wanted him to demonstrate. Soon the report
was doing exactly that, and the executive was quietly fuming
about it. He knew he'd empowered the report, but now it
annoyed him when he didn't get his way all the time.

It's just not easy. Leaders are told that they should feel
comfortable surrounding themselves with those who have
more talent. The leadership gurus all say that it's not important to be the smartest and most capable person in the room;
it's better to have the smartest and most capable team. Well, it
takes a self-confident human being, with a firm grip on his or
her position and status, to truly work that way, and I have not
met many who qualify. Leadership, after all, is about credibility. Credibility requires confidence, certainty, and capability.

Allowing others to see that you lack capability and certainty can be dangerous in the real world. Once doubts about the leader's credibility begin to form, they can be very difficult to repair. Every leader knows this, and every leader fears it.

LETTING GO

Empowering others while the leader is still ostensibly in charge is one thing; letting go of the reins completely at the time of succession is even more difficult. And that's what succession means to most leaders: the final letting go of everything that has ever moved, inspired, or meant something to them.

No wonder it's hard. Leaders get to a position of leadership because they love what they do. They think about their jobs longer, work at them harder, care more about the outcome, and identify more closely with their organizations than almost everyone else. Ever notice how hard leaders find it to take time off from work and really leave the office behind? They still talk about business decisions while playing golf or whitewater rafting. They debate strategy and tick off internal to-do lists whether they're doing yoga, making love to their spouse, lighting the candles on their child's birthday cake, or getting prepped for heart surgery. Leaders find it exceptionally hard to detach themselves from their work.

Succession planning means making leaders think about that moment when they will cease doing something significant. In truth, human beings fear a lack of significance more than almost anything else. It's death without meaning. Think about the pharaohs of ancient Egypt. From the moment they ascended to the seat of ultimate power, they began to plan for their death. When they started working on their pyramid, they aimed to make it bigger, more impregnable, and more ostentatious than any other pharaoh's pyramid. When they died, they wanted their body to be preserved as close as possible to how it had been in life. And they wanted to surround their body with all of their earthly possessions, including still-living servants who would be sacrificed to continue providing service in the great beyond. What motivated them in this regard? First, they didn't want to leave anything behind, and second, they wanted everyone to see how significant they had been in life. Behind every palace, bridge, book, movie, child, painting, pipeline, car, and rose bush, there has been a desire for creating something of significance that will outlast us when we're gone.

Shouldn't a handpicked successor be the ultimate pyramid in that sense? Yes, in theory, which is why most leaders who can face succession choose someone who resembles them closely. In fact, if genetic cloning were an available option, I bet a lot of leaders would go that route. They can be blind to seeing other options. Hard-charging, visionary entrepreneurs believe that only another hard-charging visionary entrepreneur can replace them. Chances are the organization would be better off with a soft-spoken, detail-oriented, systems thinker anyway. But few leaders can look at what mix of skills and abilities is necessary to continue their legacy because few people can see beyond the narcissism of the all-important me. In that sense, we're all Sun Kings.

YOU DON'T KNOW JACK

In a human resource dream world, succession planning would look a lot like the way it did at GE when Jack Welch stepped down after twenty years at the helm. But if we are to imagine emulating the smooth, productive, effective transition that took place at GE, we need to think less about the glossy, rosy glow of feel-good leadership and more about the messy urges underpinning human nature.

First, the results were outstanding. Jeffrey Immelt has been everything Jack Welch said he would be, and more. Despite taking over the company two weeks before the September 2001 terrorist attacks and assuming command of the ship during the first global economic recession in ten years, Immelt has been a smashing success. According to my inside sources, he could, in fact, be better than Welch. It's a coup for GE and a feather in Welch's cap.

To make that happen, Welch ran the company to great profit and market success over a tremendously challenging period of change and pitfalls. When age caught up with him and before he got sick, infirm, or distracted, Welch created a little internal contest. For years, he had been empowering leaders within the organization to run their own kingdoms. Each of these kingdoms competed with each other while simultaneously contributing to the overall bottom line. In other words, dangling the carrot of succession, Welch and GE gained terrific benefits. No doubt, the competing leaders knew they were being manipulated in this way, but why should they care about that? They were chomping at the bit to get the chance to take Jack's seat.

When speculation about succession heated up, everyone talked about the great bench strength at GE. As important as this was from a succession standpoint, it was also a very prominent feather in Welch's cap. Of course, according to the conventional wisdom, none of those people had exactly what Jack has, but collectively they were a pretty good facsimile. While I'm not saying that's what Jack Welch really believed, I am saying that he is a human being with an ego who probably didn't mind hearing such things from time to time.

When Welch finally made his choice of successor, he knew that his also-rans wouldn't stick around. Monstrous egos would be bruised; the crass, craven desire to amass power would be frustrated; and other companies, eager to benefit from GE's leadership development work, would be quick to entice those second choices to their own firms. Sure enough, that's what occurred, but something amazing happened in the process. Jack Welch's and GE's reputation only grew when three possible successors besides Immelt went on to become CEOs of other Fortune 500 firms.

In a way, Jack Welch was never really letting go of power so much as he was becoming more powerful. It's like Obi Wan Kenobi in the first Star Wars movie (the real first one, not the one that your kids think is the first one). Fighting Darth Vader, he calmly says, "If you strike me down, I shall become more powerful than you can possibly imagine." It also reminds me of John D. Rockefeller when, on the golf course, he learned the news about the forced breakup of Standard Oil. Bending over to stick his tee in the ground, he practiced his swing and said, "Well, now I'm worth three times what I was ten minutes ago."

Compare all this to the succession planning process at Disney, and you will see even more clearly how human nature gets in the way of letting go of power. After the death of his second-in-command in 1994, Michael Eisner was under some pressure to choose and groom a successor. According to James Stewart (2005), Eisner immediately thought about his old friend Michael Ovitz, whom he believed could help with some of the workload of running Disney while sending positive messages to Wall Street. There was some reservation on Eisner's part, however. As he admitted, "You have to understand, I don't want to feel as if I'm in competition with anybody" (p. 173). It is a sentiment any CEO could understand.

A few days later, Eisner felt some chest pains, and the doctors discovered he needed immediate emergency bypass surgery. Finally, with death imminent, Eisner made some clear recommendations about succession. Either Ovitz or his old boss at Paramount, Barry Diller, would be fine, he said. Then, in expression of his urge to clone himself, he added that his wife, Jane, should be named to the Disney board.

Eisner's heart surgery was a success. Having stared down death, he was a bit less excited about naming a successor. Nevertheless, his wife insisted that he could no longer bear the burden alone. It was only when Ovitz was being considered as the new head of rival Universal Studios, however, that Eisner decided that he needed him on board. Discussions of their "partnership" at the helm of Disney picked up speed, and Ovitz finally agreed to sign on. Immediately, Eisner called his biographer and said, "I think I just made the biggest mistake of my career."

In his first meeting with Eisner and the top team, both the chief financial officer and general counsel told Ovitz to his face that they would never work for him. Eisner told Ovitz that nothing could be done about it. Moving into the Disney offices, Ovitz expected to take over Frank Wells's old room but was relegated to a small space on the floor below. When he suggested a staircase be built for easier access to Eisner, he was told it would waste money. After throwing his first party as a Disney executive, Ovitz's expense was monitored closely.

In other words, in every aspect of doing his job, Ovitz was being undermined and undercut. Not surprisingly, the divorce with Disney happened only a year after he had been hired. The settlement cost Disney $140 million. And Eisner got a new ten-year contract as CEO. It wasn't before he was forced out that Robert Iger got appointed.

DID YOU EXPECT A
HAPPY GOOD-BYE?

The messiness of the Disney succession makes the details sala-
cious and newsworthy, but the experiences are much more
common than the public might think. Finding a replacement
may be a leader's most critical task, but it is probably the most
unnatural one. Why would leaders embrace succession? They
spend their careers clawing their way to the top. They are
genetically predisposed to thinking they are better, stronger,
smarter, more decisive, and more important than anyone
around them. They need that confidence to handle the pressure and complicated nature of running an organization.
Asking them to scale down their egos, relinquish their grip
on power, and willingly step aside goes against everything
that has made them successful.

No leader should walk into succession planning strategy discussions thinking that emotions will not play a complicated part in the process. No one coaching a leader should
underestimate the volatility that will be encountered. No
one tapped on the shoulder to be a successor should expect
that everything will remain fair and sunny. A proactive succession planning strategy may be the right move for leaders,
but in their hearts most will always reflect on Dylan
Thomas's words: "Do not go gentle into that good night."
(1983, p. 718).

PART FOUR

Taboos of
the Person

Secret 8

LEADERS NEED TO DEMONSTRATE
WORK-LIFE BALANCE
(NO PROBLEM; WORK IS THEIR LIFE)

When Tiger Woods turned pro in 1997, the golf world got a healthy shock. Because of his talent and potential, Tiger's amateur career had been followed with great interest, but it was expected that he would need some time and experience to adjust to the higher level of competition among the seasoned veterans of the professional tour. Nevertheless, when Tiger entered his first major, the Masters, he won by seventeen strokes. According to Tiger, he didn't even show up with his A game.

Over the next five years, Tiger was practically unstoppable, winning Professional Golf Association tournaments and majors at a rate no one had seen since the young Jack Nicklaus. Many talked about Tiger's incredible natural talent and his unique physical and mental attributes. He seemed so well suited to winning the game of golf that it was as though God had decided to design the perfect player. Tiger Woods didn't deny that he had talent, but he talked more about how much time he put into practicing. Nobody, according to Tiger, seemed to notice how many buckets of balls he hit every morning, how driven he was to refine and improve every aspect of his game, and how much mental energy he devoted to analyzing each course and determining the strategy needed to win each tournament.

During that heady period, Nike came out with a powerful commercial featuring children of all ethnicities, looking into the camera and saying, "I am Tiger Woods." The message was plain: people have amazing potential in life. But was the message honest? Sure, people have potential, but talent aside, how many of those children (and television viewers) would be inclined to devote the time, energy, discipline, and dedication that Tiger showed in order to be successful? Even other professional golfers failed in that regard. Phil Mickelson was said to have as much talent as Tiger, but people wondered whether he had the hunger and the discipline. Married with two children, Mickelson seemed too devoted to his family to show the same dedication as Tiger.

As Tiger's success continued unabated, a criticism began to grow: Tiger was too dedicated to golf; he had no balance in his life. In the eyes of those judging him, it seemed to make him a slightly lesser person and tarnished his success. The reasoning seemed to be that if only those other golfers were as one-dimensional as Tiger, they would be just as good.

Well, Tiger might say, let's see them try.

THE BALANCE ACCUSATION

In organizations, leaders often face the same kind of criticism and pressure as Tiger Woods to demonstrate better work-life balance. The accusation goes like this. A leader's success is coming at a high price, a price most healthy people won't or can't pay. The drive that "unbalanced" people exhibit presents a bad role model or an unhealthy standard that needs to be curtailed so others can be free to lead more sensible and sustainable lifestyles.

Top leaders and world-class golfers can be forgiven if they sense a conspiracy directed against them under the guise of this balance accusation. In private, they may claim that the ideal of balance is used against successful high-octane types to level the playing field and reduce a competitive advantage. Are leaders successful because they are so driven? Or would we all be better off if leaders learned to live more balanced and less unhealthy lives?

Work-life balance emerged as a key business issue in the early 1990s. Globalization brought a great deal of pressure on American businesses to become more efficient. Downsizing led to the loss of many white-collar jobs. GE, for example, shed 200,000 jobs under the early leadership of Jack Welch. For those who were left behind, there was just as much work to do, but the work had to be done by fewer people and in a much more efficient manner.

In the mid-1990s, when the economy began to take off, information technology advances gave people the ability to do more work with less labor support in a shorter time and at less cost. It sounds good in theory, but those same advances changed our lives as well. Increasingly, it became harder and harder to leave work behind. There was also a need for more labor, and organizations reached out to a more diverse group of people to cover the gap in productivity. Two groups in particular, women and newly graduated students, were brought on board, and both brought their own definition of balance with them.

Women found it tough to balance the strains of managing the family on a daily basis while maintaining high productivity and performance levels in the workplace. Children needed to be raised, groceries needed to be bought, home-work needed to be done. Other women, forgoing family for career, felt the lack. No one was too happy about it. Couldn't a better balance be achieved? HR-related initiatives like flex-time, paternal leave, and in-house day care, not to mention the technological advances that allow us to work anywhere, emerged to try to answer this cry for help.

Balance was used in a different sense by those newly graduated, newly hired young people. Businesses put such a premium on hiring talented graduates that graduates realized they were a hot commodity in a feverish marketplace. They began to demand high salaries, jumbo bonuses, and loads of perks as a way of determining where they should work. De-spite all the money and status, it wasn't enough. Remember that most of these people were in their early twenties. They'd been studying their tails off for years and were now working their tails off for long hours every day. Where was the fun and excitement of youth? Businesses responded to this call for balance by creating a new coda: work hard, play hard. They built rock climbing walls, held keg parties, created business casual, and did everything in their power to give young people a sense that they "had a life." To Generation X, having a life meant having a balance between work and fun. Scram-bling HR and personnel leaders, in collaboration with CEOs and founders who knew they had to get hip, tried to cram more of that fun into the same eighteen-hour workday to keep productivity levels high.

When the recession came, people began to complain openly about the long hours and relentless pressure. The big questions loomed: Why am I here? What am I doing with my life? Isn't there something more? Increasingly, they looked for someone to blame, and it wasn't hard to find the culprit. All along, the villain had been right in front of them: the hard-charging, take-no-prisoners, do business on the golf course, at the grandson's birthday, and in the executive toilet stall CEO or senior leader.

For years, those CEOs and senior leaders had been talking about values. Well, what about family and life values? Shouldn't the CEO or senior leader be the role model for balance between work and life? Increasingly, leaders found themselves forced to undergo a kind of balance audit. Many realized they'd better learn their children's names and take up a hobby in a hurry.

CONTRADICTIONS IN THE BALANCING ACT

We admire leaders and golfers when they are successful and are insatiably curious to learn what it takes to get to the top. We watch documentaries and Oprah interviews and read the "how I did it" books. We want to identify with those successful people, and we believe, deep inside, that they are a lot like us. We even try to be them, which is why Nike pays Tiger Woods so much money to hit its golf ball. Nike knows that millions of golfers who want to be Tiger Woods will buy that golf ball in order to get some of that Tiger mojo. Reality TV shows like *The Apprentice* allowed junior tycoons to play at being Donald Trump without understanding what it really takes to be a tycoon.

Few of us follow through on doing what is needed to emulate success. We don't have the drive; we don't make the sacrifices; we don't pay the price; we don't put in the hard work. Maybe we're just wired differently. It's easier, when we don't make it, to blame a successful person's lack of balance than it is to blame our lack of talent or our lack of time and effort.

Leaders are fundamentally unbalanced because they love what they do and they want to accomplish something important in life. That drive for significance is part of the drive for immortality. As Ernest Becker stated in his book *The Denial of Death* (1973), "Most of us are not afraid of dying so much as we are afraid of dying without having done something heroic" (p. 7). Leaders combine that fear with a love for what they do. They are preordained to put their all into their work. Although John Gartner was talking about entrepreneurs in his book, *The Hypomanic Edge: The Link Between (a Little) Craziness and (a Lot of) Success in America* (2005), he could have been talking about leaders too. Gartner described such highly driven people as meeting the diagnostic criteria for hypomania, a mild form of mania characterized by restlessness, creativity, grand ambition, euphoria, risk taking, and impulsivity. There's not much balance in that mix.

If leaders feel guilt about a lack of balance, it is usually because of external pressures. The spouse says, "Honey, you're working too hard!" The children say, "You missed my soccer game again!" The direct report complains about the relentless pressure to perform, and the colleague makes cutting jokes about insatiable drive. But the leader doesn't feel as if he or she is working too hard. The leader feels as if he or she is having fun. There's a thrill to the hunt in driving for success. A deep sense of engagement comes from always having one's mind on the job. Some people relax by talking about sports or television programs. The leader relaxes by talking about the next big project or deal. On the golf course, in the boardroom, in the restaurant, it's all encompassed in the envelope called work, and for the leader, that's okay.

In part, the difference has to do with the distinction between transactional and transformational leadership. Those
who are critical of a leader's lack of balance are thinking of
work in transactional terms. Followers say, "We're already
giving you our time and our best efforts, helping you achieve
profits and share value. What's in it for us if we give even
more?" Viewed in such a way, it's only natural to want to
draw limits and set boundaries. What's "mine" becomes my
time outside the job; what's "yours" involves what I do on the
job. If the equation is out of sync, then the desire for more
work-life balance arises. If the promise of financial compensation is not offsetting the pressure, then the individual who
is out of balance wants more time to be able to focus on
family, hobbies, or health. Naturally this creates job-related
guilt, so the employee projects the need for balance on the
leader, and the leader feels the pressure to respond accordingly. Suddenly the leader is being told to leave the office at
six and go home to read his or her children a bedtime story.
But all the leader wants to do is work.

For the leader, the work-life equation doesn't compute
that way. Ask Tiger Woods what "balance" means, and he
might answer: "Four hours a day working on my short game
balanced by four hours a day working on my long game." If
someone were to say to him, "You should be out fishing,
windsurfing, and learning another language," he might say in
return, "I just don't want to." The Tiger Woodses of the world
have a different definition of balance. Like leaders, they're
supposed to say the right things about having a balanced life,
but they don't really mean it. But to say what they really feel
is taboo.

In fact, the biggest taboo of all might be to question
whether it was just coincidence that Tiger fell off the world
number one ranking when he got married. What might have

been good for Tiger in terms of balance might not have helped his golf game in the short run. Still, for five years, he was the best golfer in the world, and, yes, he has recaptured the number one ranking again, through committed hard work and discipline. As in sports, I am hard pressed to come up with an example of someone who has achieved greatness in leadership by working nine to five.

RECALIBRATING THE EQUATION

However a leader feels about work-life balance, it's important to face reality about the issues involved. Leaders who want to block unwanted pressure and maintain an intense path or correct an imbalance that has a high cost need to recalibrate what balance means on a personal level.

When forced by the balance accusation, the first question leaders should ask themselves is: Am I healthy and happy the way I am now? One of the biggest, and most legitimate, concerns about a lack of balance is an individual's physical or mental health. Overdoing it on the work front can have serious consequences. People have heart attacks, develop depression, or drink or smoke too much. They don't take the time to exercise or relieve stress. They lose their effectiveness, become ill, or drop dead as a result. Leaders by nature focus on how others are doing and tend to neglect themselves. Instead, they need to learn how to assess their own well-being and act accordingly. For instance, every time you fly in an airplane, the flight attendant announces, "Should the cabin become depressurized for any reason, an oxygen mask will fall from the ceiling. Please put your own mask on before securing the mask of anyone traveling with you." It's good advice. The first rule of work-life balance is to look after yourself before you look after others. Make sure you are healthy, happy, and satisfied with what you are doing before you see to the needs of those around you. Only by looking after yourself can you help anyone else.

I counsel leaders not to worry about changing their work-life balance if they are essentially healthy and happy. Leaders can't allow others to calibrate their work-life balance scale. They must not allow judgmental opinions to have an impact on their own acute sense of what needs to be done. Some leaders like to burn the candle at both ends for a period of time. They go for broke. They drive people extraordinarily hard. That's what leaders do. They needn't apologize for exhibiting that leadership. It's the means by which human beings accomplish great things.

When it comes to assessing balance, the individual leader probably looks at the work-life equation through a long-range lens. It's not about getting home by six several days every week. It's about going through periods of intensity counterbalanced over time. A project might last only a few months. Tenure at the helm of a major organization might last only a few years. Why should that leader be concerned about balance during that time frame? Judged over a lifetime, there might be plenty of balance. A leader could retire early and play golf for the next ten years after working eighteen-hour days for the ten years prior. A leader could become devoted to an entirely different endeavor later, providing a personal sense of balance. Or maybe the leader knows he or she will never care about balance. As one highly driven leader once said to me, "You get to sleep a long time when you're dead."

But that's the leader: the one who gains all the transformational benefits of leadership. What about the follower, the one who may receive only transactional benefits? Shouldn't we stop leaders from inflicting their own perverse sense of balance on followers to save those people from the pressure and strain of an unhealthy life? Like most other big questions, the answer is relative. Not everyone wants work-life balance, even if they say they do.

Work-life balance isn't an issue in many situations, and it's worth looking at some examples to understand why. Imagine a National Football League coach succumbing to a call for more balance. No coach, owner, player, fan, or ticket taker expects balance to enter into consideration when it comes to winning on the field. When coaches aren't coaching, they're analyzing game film. When players aren't running drills or lifting weights, they're studying playbooks. Everyone understands that the object is to win the game, and it doesn't matter how much is sacrificed to achieve that goal. Armies view balance the same way. While a soldier may be concerned about family life and extracurricular activities during peace time, when a war is being fought, no sacrifice is too great.

The trick, it would seem, is to be clear about expectations up front. If your organization does not value balance, say so. GM, the car manufacturer, was clear in its early days that hard work was more important than balance. Legend has it that managers were watched as they approached their cars on a Friday to make sure that they were carrying their briefcases. Anyone leaving a briefcase in the office probably wasn't working hard enough. Similarly, no one joins Goldman Sachs with the illusion of having a life of balance. Goldman Sachs employees complain less about work-life balance than most other professional service firms I know of despite the firm's intense and driven work culture, because no promises are made concerning balance. Few law firms, entrepreneurial ventures, or self-employed businesses want to hire employees who want work-life balance. Pfizer, however, has a clear mandate for a healthy lifestyle. This leads the organization to encourage its employees to seek a balance between work and outside interests.

Perhaps the time has come for a new philosophy about the balance issue. We live in a society where technology makes work-life balance an issue. People who don't want balance can work anytime and anywhere they want. People who do want balance can find themselves afflicted by work and unable to put up a barrier to safeguard their personal lives. But is time the best measure of an individual employee's productivity? In the industrial age, the number of hours spent on the job corresponded directly with productivity. In a knowledge economy, we should be able to focus on an individual's output and performance to assess whether he or she is sufficiently productive.

In a mature organization, the individual should be able to make an assumption about how much work-life balance is necessary for him or her personally. I am reminded of the saying at McKinsey & Co., the consulting firm. No one would ever accuse McKinsey of coddling its people, and yet the firm recognizes that individuals function best when they are accountable for themselves. New recruits are eager to do what it takes to fit in. Some firms make it clear that new employees need to throw their personal lives away for the next five or ten years. At McKinsey, however, they are told to "make your own McKinsey." In other words, it's important for individuals to assess what they want to do with their careers and live that life accordingly. Of course, no one would be kept on who didn't fulfill the requirements of the job. But top performance is not measured by a strict code of how one needs to work to get ahead. Rather, individuals determine that code for themselves and achieve top performance as a result. If they don't, no amount of working overtime will help counter an assessment of their worth.

Those who care about work-life balance should test their company to see how far they can go in moving the chains. If the organization embraces your definition, wonderful. If the organization doesn't respond in the right way, it's probably not the right place for you.

THE CREDIBLE LEADER

Credibility is critical for leaders. Accusations that a leader demonstrates poor work-life balance are dangerous because they can lead to doubt in the leader. If a human resource or public relations department claims the organization values work-life balance but the leader doesn't function that way, the leader's credibility will suffer no matter how consistently he or she is acting. No leader should have to please everyone. But naysayers will question the leader openly if they are given the opportunity to do so.

In the same way, it is dangerous for leaders if they feel personal doubt about their own approach to leading. Anyone can become confused or disoriented about the larger picture when focused on the moment-by-moment aspects of the game. Social, organizational, or familial pressure to demonstrate more work-life balance can knock leaders back if they are not aware of what balance really means to them personally.

It is critical for leaders to have a position about work-life balance and live and lead accordingly. A lack of balance may be taboo right now, but leaders have generally been people with more drive, vision, and passion than balance. Jack and Suzy Welch write eloquently in *Winning* (Welch and Welch, 2005) about the need for more work-life balance, but they themselves certainly didn't appear to practice or promote balance in their careers, although they are enjoying the fruits of their labor now. Indeed, as the Welches would be the first to admit, leadership is a process by which a leader gets the most out of people for a sustained period of time, no matter what it takes. Bearing that in mind, maybe balance is part of the equation when considering the long-term goals of the leader. Or maybe the leader knows that people will move on, and it is the leader's obligation to get the most out of them in the short term and obtain new people for the next leg of the journey. Either way, the leader needs to have a position on balance. As in other aspects of leadership, there can be no cognitive dissonance or gap between what a leader wants or needs from people and how he or she goes about obtaining it.

10

Secret 9

BLATANT SELF-INTEREST
IS DANGEROUS
(IN FOLLOWERS, NOT LEADERS)

The different business eras can be distinguished readily by the slogans that get attached to them. In the 1980s, it was greed is good, as Wall Street types became the icons of capitalism and Ronald Reagan labeled ketchup a vegetable. In the 1990s, it was anything goes, as CEOs, Internet start-up founders, and President Clinton experienced huge booms and busts in popularity and power. And in the 2000s, with a born-again President Bush and a hangover from the excesses of the roaring 1990s, it's all about ethics, integrity, and values.

Some pollsters say President Bush beat Democratic challenger John Kerry because he was most clearly identified with strong moral values. This sense that values are the new trend extends beyond politics too. Mighty businesses have fallen, we're told, because of their leaders' ethical violations. Faith and prayer are entering the workplace as more businesses deem it not only acceptable but inspirational to be open about religious beliefs.

Values have exerted pressure on company earnings reports too. After two decades of short-term thinking by CEOs regarding profits and shareholder value, some investors are proposing that an organization be held accountable for a broader range of considerations. The so-called triple bottom line is a movement to evaluate a company's worth by its impact not just on financial profits but on society and the environment too. Meanwhile, one of the big trends in leadership development is something called servant leadership. According to proponents, it's no longer enough for CEOs to be stewards of their company's vision, competitive strategy, and profitability; they also need to be ethical purists who serve the betterment of employees.

Taken together, it's not hard to believe that a transformation is going on. But one has to question whether the slogans and buzzwords actually mean anything in terms of how a leader does the job. In the real world, do values matter more than profits? Should leaders put aside their own motivations and interests and serve only the motivations and interests of their people?

The answer, in my view, is short but sweet: sometimes leaders are motivated by the greater good, but usually that's by accident. Values are wonderful things for a company, *if* it gets a leader what he or she really wants. In other words, despite the veneer of ethics, not much has truly changed in our leaders because the essential dynamic of leadership remains the same. Leadership is rooted in the urges of blatant self-interest. Fortunately, to paraphrase Wall Street raider Gordon Gekko in the movie *Wall Street* (1987), blatant self-interest is good. How come nobody says that openly? Why, of course, it's taboo.

ETHICAL DILEMMAS

Martha Stewart did time in jail. Investment banker Frank Quattrone got his sentence too. Dennis Kozlowski was a poor boy from Newark who made good, becoming the fabulously rich CEO of Tyco. Now he's a poor boy from Newark serving time. Jeffrey Skilling was such a wunderkind at McKinsey that Enron hired him to be its president. Now his name is associated with colossal scandal.

All of these top-flight leaders and others share one thing in common: they are guilty of ethics violations. Kellerman, in *Bad Leadership* (2004), notes that we prefer to ignore such taboo breakers as random bad apples rather than individuals who embody aspects of leadership that are not pretty. She asks, "How will we ever stop what we refuse to see and study?" But in searching for an antidote to these bad apples, we need to be careful that we don't create yet another layer of myth around leadership. An executive or manager who is going to be effective in that role better understand what leadership really takes. To that point, here's a news flash: being the nicest, kindest, most generous, spiritual, thoughtful, and caring person in the world does not make anyone the greatest leader. In fact, the most effective leaders tend to be the ones who do whatever it takes to achieve their own very selfish agenda. If that happens to overlap with your needs, great. If not, you'd better get out of their way.

Am I saying that ethics and leadership are like oil and water and effective leaders are cruel, selfish, and manipulative? Not a chance. For the record, I think that ethical conduct is good business. Corporations can be unethical hotbeds.

People inside them can lie, cheat, steal, racially discriminate, and sexually harass, just as in any other social environment. Ethics provides a standard for conduct that facilitates good teamwork, effective execution, and decent treatment of employees and customers.

In fact, it's the impact of ethics that provides insight into why it really matters. Herb Kelleher, chairman of Southwest Airlines, believes deeply in the principle of reciprocity. He thinks that you should treat people with respect, kindness, and decency because that's a model and standard for how you want people to treat others, including yourself. To Kelleher, reciprocity is like the Golden Rule times three. Do unto others as you would have them do unto you because that's probably how they'll do unto each other and your customers too. Kelleher, it shouldn't surprise you, is also big on honesty. He believes in treating people well, creating a humane workplace, and being responsive to human needs. Does that make Herb Kelleher a candidate for sainthood? Far from it. Kelleher is no one's poster child for religious figuredom. He parties hard, drinks, and enjoys a hand of high-stakes black-jack once in a while. But ask his people what they think of him, and you'll get a clear answer: "He'd go through a brick wall for me, and I'd go through one for him."

That's one of the secrets to Kelleher's leadership success. As a leader, he is able to generate tremendous loyalty, caring, diligence, and top performance, all at a discount price. He also gains leadership credibility by getting results, breaking the industry mold, showing profitability quarter after quarter, and kicking the stuffing out of his competitors. But since we're talking about values, let's stick to the ethical side of the equation. Does Kelleher act that way to employees because he's just a wonderful, ethical kind of guy, or does he act that way because he knows what results his behavior will get from others?

My question is, should it really matter? I believe firmly that Kelleher acts the way he does out of personal principle. He couldn't do it so effectively if it weren't an authentic expression. But are there moments when Herb Kelleher would rather get his foot stuck in a bear trap than be nice to someone? I bet there are plenty of days like that. As a leader, however, Kelleher probably sucks it up, nine times out of ten, and keeps his warm, friendly, outgoing persona in place. He's big on the Golden Rule and other ethical principles not because the Bible tells him so, but because it's good for business. Does that make him a hypocrite? In my book, it makes him a smart, effective leader.

ESPN is another organization that prides itself on creating a positive work environment. When people needed day care, it put in day care service. When they needed flextime and work-from-home capability, it instituted that too. On top of that, it built a wonderful cafeteria and a fantastic gym. Throw in the fact that you've got sports on television monitors and radios all over the place, and it sounds more like a country club than a corporate office. So why did management do it? Was there any expectation that they might get a little more out of employees this way? You're right. It's all part of the transactional quality of leadership. If you build a million-dollar gym for your employees, it needs to provide a certain return on investment in order to make rational business sense.

In other words, ethics and values need to be part of the business equation in business terms. If you're the head of an oil refinery, it may be cheaper in the short run to cut corners on safety, but if you're thinking about the sustainability of your business in the medium to long term, you'd better make safety a big priority. Imagine the fallout if a pipeline company had a spill near a city or a wetland. Environmental stewardship and community responsibility may sound like an ethical or moral principle, but it's just as much a business principle.

In fact, I bet that any great leader in an industry where safety and environmental concerns loom large is particularly passionate about those issues. It's Darwinian in that sense, since a competitive company in that market would select such qualities in its leaders. Think of Eileen Fisher. As the head of one of the country's most successful women's clothing companies, she's obsessive in her anti–sweat shop stance and also works hard every day to make sure that her people have the opportunity for stress relief in the form of yoga, flextime, meditation, and substantial community involvement. Some leaders might think this is a waste of time and resources, but for Fisher, her passions and concerns overlap with the passions and concerns of her employees and customers. People look good wearing her clothes, and they also feel good about the label; together, this gives her a competitive advantage in securing the hearts and minds of her customers in a fickle industry.

IF I HAD A MILLION DOLLARS

Still, some CEOs and company founders inevitably get to the point where money and power don't seem to matter anymore. They've got more than they could ever spend and plenty more coming in. They've been ruthlessly competitive all their lives. It's time to give back. Sheehy talks about that in her book *New Passages* (1995). At a later stage in their careers, powerful and successful people decide to give back.

Sheehy recognizes that this is part of generativity—a primal urge to replicate themselves in others. In other words, there is still plenty of self-interest involved in the decision to be more giving.

There are plenty of examples. George Soros, who bet against the English pound and made $1 billion at the expense of the British government, puts a ton of money into various causes around the world, including immigration issues in the United States and democracy promotion in Eastern Europe. In his books, he often rails against the evils of unfettered capitalism. Warren Buffett, history's most successful investor, is also one of our era's most generous philanthropists, and he has frequently gone on record as complaining that tax cuts and corporate loopholes benefit the super-rich like himself at the expense of ordinary people. Oprah Winfrey has taken her fame and the wealth she created through her business, Harpo Enterprises, to shed light on and address the disease and strife in Africa. Bill Gates was criticized severely earlier in his career for not doing enough for charity. Now, the Bill and Melinda Gates Foundation is a major global force in health and education issues.

Why do they do it? Some people look at such largesse and think, *Finally these people have seen the light.* They've been focused on money obsessively all their lives, and now they realize they can't take it with them. It's time to spread some crumbs around.

True, there's some evidence for that kind of cynical position. Most of the super-wealthy philanthropists didn't do much to distinguish themselves as generous givers earlier in their careers. But does that mean they are atoning for past sins?

I would argue that successful philanthropists are leaders who recognize that the sphere of their influence has changed.

They make a rational assessment of the time and energy they put into their companies and compare that to the impact they could have on outside interests. Where that impact is a better investment, they turn their attention to it and apply those same skills and behaviors that make them effective as business leaders on a social mission. Bill Gates, for instance, looks at what a half-day and $10 million of his time working for Microsoft will do, and compares that to what $10 million will do for distributing vaccines in Africa. When he can really feel that his power and impact will be expressed, his philanthropic inclinations tip the balance over his business inclinations, and he goes into action.

Am I saying that Bill Gates and George Soros do their good work for more power and influence? Maybe. I am certain that it does not hurt their power and influence, and it surely helps to satisfy their passion. Leaders think differently from most of the rest of us about such matters. In fact, it's a distinction that's worth examining. As opposed to the measured and strategic approach of Bill Gates or George Soros, there are leaders who go overboard in pursuit of noble causes. Think of Jimmy Carter and his all-consuming quest for Middle East peace. Carter, a religious man, no doubt felt a moral calling and spiritual obligation to use his power and influence for the greatest possible good. But was that really the best use of his power and influence? By focusing so exclusively on one aspect of his job, there was a feeling that he let other aspects go by the wayside. Maybe if he'd been a more effective and diligent president on other issues, he might have won a second term, affording him more power and influence in the process. Mother Teresa was a selfish leader in the sense that her agenda was incredibly important to her, but her pursuit of that agenda was for the greater good.

Whether leaders are effective in their philanthropic or noble pursuits is all part of the equation. When they lose sight of that formula, they should probably rethink their goals and motivations. It might be time for them to resign their position and take on a new role in life.

THE ETHICAL TOOL KIT

Being a leader is not about being a force for good, although much good can come from leadership. Instead, morality, ethics, and principles are tools that leaders use to be more effective.

President George W. Bush did not come into office to serve the needs of the Christian right who voted for him. He came into office to serve his own needs and used the Christian right as a means of achieving his goal. In fulfilling his agenda during his second term, there will be occasions when he also fulfills their agenda but not because he is their servant leader. Should the people who voted for Bush because of his values feel betrayed? Not at all. They have used some of their power and influence to achieve their agenda too.

Blatant self-interest is the way of leaders. Stephen Covey, in his book *The Eighth Habit* (2004), talks about the importance of a leader's identifying his or her passion. In my view, passion could be translated as blatant self-interest. It's not about crossing ethical boundaries; it means that what's important to a leader drives his or her work ethic and goals. Everyone would acknowledge that when leaders pursue their own passion, or blatant self-interest, they are more powerful, and the likelihood of their success goes up dramatically. Is this good or bad? At times, a leader's blatant self-interest may be in parallel with the mission and values of the company. At other times, that self-interest may be at cross-purposes with the organization's needs. At such times, as writers like Barbara Kellerman have pointed out, leaders can often go horribly astray in pursuit of their own interests. But maybe if leaders felt more comfortable to discuss true feelings and beliefs about self-interest, there would be more checks and balances along the way. Others could support or criticize the leader's aims accordingly. As Robert J. Samuelson noted in his article "No Joke: CEO's Do Some Good" (2005), "The true transformation of CEO's is not the plunge from grace. It's a slow evolution that, despite excesses and mistakes, has served us well . . ." (p. 49).

Blatant self-interest doesn't always translate into good business. Fortunately, it often does, and it benefits a lot of people in the process. Leadership is about getting the most out of people for as long as possible in order to achieve one's goals. In today's economy, people are free to work for anyone they like, including themselves. They don't have to follow any old leader; they can choose to follow a leader who provides the kind of work environment they want. In that sense, leaders who are ethical understand that those characteristics give them a competitive advantage over others. They use all the tools at their disposal to be more effective, and ethics is one of those tools.

11

Secret 10

IT'S LONELY AT THE TOP (BUT LEADERS WOULDN'T HAVE IT ANY OTHER WAY)

What's not to like about leadership? Being at the top means getting all the attention and all the perks. Not only are all eyes on you, but you still get away with behavior that no one else is allowed even to think about trying. You receive more than your share of respect, credibility, and authority just by virtue of your position. You are able to assert your will over others to get things done. People march to the drum of your beat, not the other way around. To top it all off, even though this kind of approach to life might be termed selfish or self-centered at home, blatant self-interest is considered a good thing in the leadership arena.

Sure, you have to work hard, and there's a lot of responsibility and demands. You don't have a clue what this so-called work-life balance thing means. Your health and relationships often suffer, and your personal interests are generally limited to a narrow scope of activities and pursuits that feed your business. Yeah, you'll probably have a little trouble giving up your leadership role gracefully. And, yes, it really sucks that you'll be forced to go through the motions of picking and grooming a successor, something that feels about as good as choosing your spouse's new love interest. But given all that, the power, privilege, and prestige of leadership are still alluring carrots. Again, you have to ask: What's not to like?

Should it surprise you that the leader experiences great loneliness too? At many times during the daily routine and certainly at the end of a long career, it is the leader who is most clearly and irrevocably left alone. For many people, this is the hardest and most unexpected aspect of being a leader. Of course, they don't talk about it or acknowledge it. But you know why already: the loneliness of leadership is a taboo.

THE LEADERSHIP HANGOVER

Being a successful leader is a bit like being an alcoholic or a gambling addict. There comes a time when the party stops or a lull sets in, and the leader experiences a leadership hangover. In a very real sense, the leader is addicted to being a leader.

Doctors know that addiction is powerful because it is physical, not just psychological. An addiction occurs when your body is so used to getting an external high that it demands you keep feeding it. The natural dopamine in your body goes to sleep as long as that external stimulus keeps coming in. When that stimulus stops, your body rushes to reproduce the effect naturally, a physical change that hurts. Such pain is what those of us who have ever had too much to drink call a hangover.

Drinkers can get addicted to alcohol. Runners can get addicted to running. Office workers can get addicted to diet soft drinks or Internet porn. Soccer moms can get addicted to diet pills or quick-pick lottery tickets. Rock stars and professional athletes can get addicted to cheering crowds. Leaders can get addicted to leading.

If you want to think about leadership addiction in a comparative way, try Las Vegas. There are no clocks in the casino, so you have no sense of time and no awareness of any limits. The drinks are free. The colored lights and chiming bells are dazzling. The casino staff and the pretty cocktail waitress gives you lots of attention, and the dealer is not only polite and deferential but treats you with respect. You're sitting around a table with a group of peers, all of you engrossed in the game. There's a sense of risk and high stakes, a thrill of winning and a fear of losing. Your focus gets incredibly intense, and you block out everything around you. That's okay, though, because everyone you're sitting with is doing the same thing. You're all trying to beat the odds, win the game, and pile up the rewards. The intensity of competition is coursing through your blood.

Of course, those other gamblers around the table aren't really your friends, but they understand your interests better than anyone else at that moment, and they share your sense of competition and concentration. Okay, so the cocktail waitress is being flirty and cheerful only because she depends on your good mood for tips, and the dealer doesn't respect you as much as he or she respects your money. And, yes, the free drinks, long hours, and lack of exercise are taking its toll on your physical well-being.

Now imagine that the power goes out, the curtain goes up, the daylight streams in, and you discover that it's noon, on some unknown day, and your spouse and dog have left you.

Leaders don't have a lot of balance in their lives. They don't seek much outside work for stimulation. Their friends tend to be work friends, sometimes on their side, sometimes in competition—fellow gamblers whose real lives are often unknown. When the job stops, they feel emotionally and physically spent.

LEADERSHIP IS NOT A DAY JOB

For most people, work is a job. For leaders, it's much much more.

Roger Goodell, the commissioner of the NFL, conducted an employee satisfaction survey when he was chief operating officer to gauge how happy his people were with their jobs. One of the general issues brought up among junior employees went something like this: "At times we're made to feel that we're lucky to work at the NFL. Whenever we raise concerns, we are listened to but also reminded that the NFL is a great place to work."

When I discussed this with Goodell, he was both surprised and animated. To him, working for the NFL *is* a great place to work. He feels lucky every day he comes to work, and he thinks that every employee should share that same sense of wonder and enthusiasm. For Goodell, working at the NFL is the coolest thing he could ever imagine doing; there's no other organization like it in the world. He simply can't understand why every single other person doesn't feel the same way. Clearly the club owners also recognized this when they named Goodell to succeed Paul Tagliabue as their eighth league chief executive in August 2006.

For the record, I can't understand it either. The NFL *is* the coolest place I could imagine working for. But Goodell's comments are not unusual ones for leaders, no matter where they work, whether that is the NFL or the Acme Bolt Cutting Company.

Leaders are separated from followers by what drives them, a distinction that is the source of some degree of loneliness. Leaders have a greater sense of urgency than their followers. They are more active about seeing and doing something about problems and opportunities. They care more about outcomes. They cherish the opportunity to make a difference through accomplishing their objectives.

Followers say that it is natural for leaders to have a bigger sense of emotional investment in the organization. After all, the leader is the one who benefits most when the organization succeeds. If the followers had as much at stake and could gain as much as the leader, they'd care that much too.

In fact, this simply doesn't bear out. As leadership studies have shown, a leader is someone who cares more, even when he or she is still a junior executive and not in a position of any authority. Some people argue that this is why they become leaders. Their caring, passion, and effort go a long way to distinguishing them on the job at every rung of the ladder.

Leaders can't understand why someone would not want to spend all of his or her time thinking about work, on and off the job. They don't get the person who has to go off fishing or mountain hiking or to the opera to feel good about life.

Eventually this sense of disconnect begins to have an impact on leaders. Not only do they feel lonely in the crowd, but they come to use that aloneness as a psychological tool. After all, leaders often have to make tough decisions. Sometimes they have to fire a friend or give a poor performance rating. Sometimes they have to close a factory or lead an army into battle. Being put into that position is lonely, but it's also easier if one is alone. It would cloud anyone's judgment to have strong emotional ties to the people whose fates are being decided. Leaders can have trouble getting good data. The people around them are eager to tell them what they want to hear. It's easy to fall into the trap of sycophancy, if only because it masks the loneliness. And yet a leader needs distance from others in order to be effective.

Leaders use the mystique of power both to maintain status and motivate others. Getting close to the leader is a game among followers, inspiring a kind of performance competition. Shrewd leaders play this game very skillfully, knowing that the cost of the game is their own further isolation. A successful senior executive I know loved to play golf. Outside of work, it was his one true enjoyment and passion. To please him and get time with him, his key reports periodically organized golf outings. To be one of those key three or seven people on a regular outing was a sign of status in the division. But the executive knew that he couldn't let his guard down and get too close to these people regardless of the human dimension of the activity. It would impair his effectiveness as their leader.

He understood that leaders cultivate loneliness deliberately.

THE GREATEST NEED

Being exceptional or unique is never as easy as one might suppose, no matter what the circumstances. Just as the world's tallest or heaviest man feels fundamentally alone, so does the world's best tennis player and the smartest kid in a classroom. While accolades, attention, or achievements might seem to mitigate that loneliness, the sense of distinction can actually exacerbate it.

The French medieval philosopher Nicole said that the greatest need of all human beings is to be understood; the second is to understand. Leaders are prone to understand others well. They try to understand the character of the people who work for them. They look for the emotional triggers that will motivate a person to greater performance. They do so from a certain distance.

Followers are not so prone to understand leaders. They try to read a leader's moods and anticipate his or her decisions, but they do so from a perspective that rarely allows them to see the entire picture. They tend to objectify the leader and interpret him or her from a more institutional stance than a human one.

If Nicole is right, then this puts leaders in a bind. They have very few people they can turn to for understanding. No wonder elite leadership has become a kind of sequestered club. No one understands or can relate to the concerns of a CEO better than another CEO, even when they are rivals. I am reminded of the great chess master Kasparov and his relationship with his rival, Karpov. The two men hated each other. They were on opposite sides of the political fence at a very tense political time. Their egos drove each to disdain the other even as it motivated them to better play. But when Kasparov was asked why he spent so much solitary time with Karpov, a man he hated, he replied, "Who else in the world can I talk to about chess?" President Bush jokes that Bill Clinton is his dad's second son, referring to the friendship and collaboration of his father and Clinton.

In the end, a leader is alone. Unfortunately, a lot of leaders don't recognize this until it confronts them in some dramatic personal way. For years, they have pushed aside any feelings of loneliness because the addiction of leadership satisfies so many needs. Like the concern for work-life balance, they have a tendency to calibrate loneliness and the importance of intimate relationships on a different scale from most of us. Just as some people don't realize that they have clogged arteries or high cholesterol until physical illness befalls them, so a leader may not understand the extent of this loneliness until some life crisis occurs.

Sometimes that crisis comes in a career shift. Maybe they have retired or been passed over for the CEO position or taken a fall in some high-level political gamesmanship. Sometimes the crisis is physical. A heart attack or cancer, for example, can lead anyone to assess what really matters in life and where they stand in that regard. Sometimes the crisis is personal, as an important relationship with a family member, spouse, child, or dear friend causes pain. And sometimes the crisis can even come through success. When the pinnacle of power has been reached, the money and accolades toted up, and all the other players around the blackjack table are out of chips, a feeling of "What next?" can set in, and with it comes a deep melancholy.

Loneliness is so rarely talked about because it implies vulnerability, something that is anathema to leaders. But for the individual, the onset of loneliness can make for a grim last decade or so or a series of attempts to fill in the emptiness through adventure, excitement, or a new, and younger, spouse. Their leadership reaches a higher plane, and they become less energized but wiser. They stay engaged in ways that give them an opportunity for creative expression and assertion of willpower—those acts that give life a sense of meaning according to the existential philosophers.

It's too bad we can't learn more from such people. But the entire discussion of loneliness is off-limits. We can't seem even to acknowledge the issues, let alone deal with them. The intimate feelings can be embarrassing and the privileged position of the sufferer more worthy of satire than sympathy. But for those considering a leadership path and those fully immersed and engaged in the leadership game, it is critical to face all the leadership taboos, and loneliness is one of them.

12

Our Taboos Are Exposed, So Now What?

In March 2005, when *NYPD Blue* finally went off the air after ten seasons, the ratings for its last show didn't come close to denting its competitor that night, *American Idol*. Instead of watching a serious drama with serious actors, audiences preferred the acerbic comments of some British judge on reality TV. What's so great about hearing Simon tell some poor kid singing "My Way" that she's got a voice like a cat in a blender? I think the power of the show arises because he's violating the taboo that says, "Thou shalt not be honest when someone has no talent." We get a tingle of pleasure from hearing the truth.

Of course, no one would accuse reality TV of actually being real. We all know the dialogue and confrontations are contrived, reshot, and edited. In fact, everything about such programs seems staged and unreal. But the people on the shows are not actors, and we can relate to their real emotions. Watching through our television screens provides a voyeuristic experience, up close and titillating while also safe. To me, that mode of viewing only confirms the power of taboos. We're not really breaking them when we watch TV. The pleasure comes from watching real people squirm and knowing that no harm will come to us. If you've ever seen a live performance or a public incident in which taboos really get broken, you'll know the difference. The experience can be very uncomfortable and anxiety inducing.

That's why, when I read that "reality" is making a comeback in corporate America, I have certain doubts. Plenty of recent articles and books hit the issue right on the head, but do they understand why there is a problem in the first place? An article in *Fortune* in 2002, "Why Companies Fail," established some of the basic tenets. According to authors Ram Charan and Jerry Unseem, companies fail for a lot of reasons, including the fact that CEOs are sometimes too intimidating to be truthful with; organizational cultures have a tendency to ignore rather than confront the brutal facts. Larry Bossidy and Charan then hit the issue again in their best-selling book, *Confronting Reality* (2004). Bossidy and Charan suggest that many leaders are lost in self-perpetuation illusions and fail to confront the real issues of business. Their book provides a model for facing facts that are external and internal to the company and shows how managers who do this succeed, while those who don't fail. The fact that the 2005 *Harvard Business Review* list of "Breakthrough Ideas for 2005" included, as idea number thirteen, "A Taboo on Taboos" was a cry to acknowledge and deal with various elephants in the room. Every company has serious issues that everyone ignores because they are taboo. As the authors wrote, "The challenge is to enable full and frank discussions of touchy topics without creating a hostile environment" (Buchanan, p. 43).

I couldn't agree more. But acknowledging that challenge is like saying that voyages to other galaxies would be great; we just need to get there. In other words, I'm not arguing that articles and books exhorting us to confront reality aren't on target; my concern is that there's a difference between knowing that something exists and facing up to it. If it were easy to face reality, wouldn't we be doing so already?

We avoid confronting reality, acknowledging elephants, and facing brutal facts because that helps us to avoid the painful social anxiety we feel when breaking a taboo. It's very easy to watch Simon on *American Idol* skewer talentless wretches on national television. It's very difficult for a wife to tell her husband, "Actually, honey, I do think you look sort of fat in that suit. Maybe you should work out a bit more and maybe it is also time to look into a Rogaine treatment for your thinning hair?" Similarly, it's easy to read about companies that have made terrible strategic errors because they haven't been able to face an obvious problem. But it's very difficult to speak up in a meeting or walk into your boss's office and speak such truths. Sometimes we'd rather ignore the elephant than risk the embarrassment, exposure, or anxiety of pointing out something that is obvious but socially sensitive.

What helps to dilute that power is acknowledging that it exists. Knowing that there are taboos and knowing why that makes them difficult to discuss provides us with a bit of ammunition. It's like taking off our clothes at the doctor's office. Nobody likes to sit there in one of those backless paper gowns, but until we strip, the doctor can't help us.

That's what this book has been about. By exposing the taboos that we may run into during the course of our working lives, we give ourselves the opportunity to see reality, perhaps for the first time. For this last effort in that task, let's look at some of the taboos we've discussed so far and see what we can do about them.

ATTACKING TABOOS

I believe that taboos either serve a purpose or once served a purpose. Originally it was wise not to eat pork because illness from poorly cooked pork was potentially deadly; today, the taboo retains cultural significance. Once, showing disrespect to the monarch was punishable by immediate execution; today, we recognize that such behavior was forbidden because threats to the fragile social order could be devastating. In similar ways, many of the taboos that exist in corporate America served very real purposes historically. Although some of those taboos are still functional, others serve a secondary cultural function, and still others hang around without any legitimate purpose and may even be harmful.

As most of us know, it's important to be respectful of history and even cherish it, but history can also be stifling and oppressive to the living. So it goes with taboos, some of which are still with us out of respect for culture and tradition; others because they hang around like old vines that strangle new growth.

What Leadership Takes

Leadership is one of the most observed and studied phenomena on earth, yet it is poorly understood. It has become all things to all people, which has given way to the misconception that anyone can do it if given the chance. As a result, followers fail to appreciate what it really takes, and leaders have come to resent followers for not understanding. Followers also feel a bit slighted given the fact that most leaders make more than 500 percent than they do, not to mention all the perks.

Make no mistake about it, leadership entails major sacrifice. It takes incredible amounts of skill and even more will. In some ways, leading is an unnatural act. Years ago, I heard of a study (that I never validated) that seemed to make a lot of sense concerning leadership. A researcher apparently studied the difference between a school of fish and the lead fish. Time after time, the story goes, the researcher discovered that what differentiated the lead from the school was that the leader was slightly brain damaged. My mother, years ago, taught gifted kids and emotionally disabled kids, and she always said they were one and the same. The bottom line is that leadership takes more than what most people have or are willing to give up. The amount of skill required is shocking, but the amount of will is mind-boggling. If we are ever to help individuals and organizations develop leadership, we must be brave enough to confront its reality.

Charisma

Is it really necessary to be charismatic? Although it may be politically incorrect to say so, having a certain something still seems to matter. I remember a meeting I had with a CEO who was talking about the difficulties he was having in considering a junior executive for promotion. "He's smart, he's capable, and he wants to run the division, but he just doesn't have it." I asked the CEO if "it" meant charisma. He said, "I don't know if that's what I'm talking about, but when you see him with investors and analysts, you realize that people don't respond to him. There's a lack of personal impact. I wish it wasn't the case, but I can't pretend it's not a problem."

The CEO's reservations can't be dismissed too quickly. The divisional position, one of five in the company, was important for grooming a successor. To award that position to someone who deserved it but didn't have potential as a successor would be a waste. Still, to explain that to the junior executive would be to risk creating very bad feelings. But was the CEO's poorly articulated sense of what the junior executive was lacking really so important? Could he have demonstrated charisma in different ways? Could he have relied on different strengths to compensate? Although subjective and intangible, charisma is a commodity like any other leadership trait. We should be able to talk about it.

Politics

What's wrong with playing politics? Political behavior exists in organizations because organizations are social phenomena. To succeed in them, you have to know how to play certain games. But a preponderance of political behavior can also divert valuable attention and focus to game playing. Where should the onus fall?

The problem with downplaying political behavior is that it does happen, and it is necessary. To tell a developing leader that he or she will have more integrity by avoiding being political is naive and bad advice. Such a person will be disadvantaged on the way up, allowing others who may have less to offer to succeed ahead of him or her. And yet it's also critical that leaders be ethical in their behavior. In that sense, too, it's necessary to let young leaders know when and how being political can cross a line. If we ignore politics as a nasty dark side of corporate life that we'd like to pretend doesn't exist, does that do the organization any favors?

Gender

Talking about gender differences can get a leader, especially a male leader, in big trouble. But not talking about gender differences can be detrimental to an organization. In aggregate, people of different gender can have different goals and different expectations for their work environment. Even if this isn't true, such subsurface perceptions can have an impact on reality.

Leadership is a function of skill and will. I think that every study, and every executive's personal experience will show, that there are no gender differences in skill. In fact, when it comes to the new leadership science of emotional intelligence, women are often perceived to be more skilled than men. But it is the experience of many male executives I know that women have less will to lead. Is this impression fair to a woman who wants to lead as much as a man? In my view, if a woman does have the will, chances are she'll ultimately get there. But I concede that the impediments may hold back lots of women whose will is the same as that of men but no greater. Wouldn't we all be better off if women and men could put their cards on the table and know exactly what everyone in the room is thinking? If you don't know what I mean, ask Lawrence Summers, the ex-president of Harvard University.

The Double Standard

As Charan and Unseem argue in "Why Companies Fail" (2002), one of the reasons given for failure is that people can find the boss too intimidating to approach with unpleasant truths. We all know that authority is intimidating. But most of us don't realize that people in authority are also reluctant to bring truth to those below them for the same reason. Or as Jack Nicholson, playing a cantankerous general on trial in the movie *A Few Good Men,* said: "You can't handle the truth!"

As a manifestation of that problem, we often say that an organization has a lack of transparency in its top ranks. Another way of describing it is to criticize a leader for saying one thing and doing another. Usually when we point to the old D.A.I.S.N.A.I.D. (do as I say . . .) phenomenon, we're expressing bitterness that the boss gets away with something that the masses could never hope to.

As I've already discussed in this book, many people in authority are just fine with the double standard because they think they deserve it. Organizations may be meritocracies for those on the way up, but that doesn't mean that all rewards should be handed out equally. There are good arguments for providing top executives with more perks and privileges than others. But those arguments are unlikely to be made by executives; they're scared to discuss such matters openly. I don't see that changing soon, but I do think employees should be more aware of how hard executives work and how much they sacrifice.

Playing Favorites

Leaders are supposed to treat everyone equally regardless of worth, output, or sense of personal connection. But is that realistic or even positive? You'd have to be a pretty bloodless person not to feel more connection with some people over others. And in a strict cost-benefit analysis, isn't it wise for a leader to devote more time and effort to those who have the greatest potential?

Of course, the detriments are real. A leader who is too reliant on favorites can shut himself or herself off from the world and become surrounded by sycophantic sidekicks. It's also true that it can be difficult and frustrating for top performers to succeed in an organization heavy with favoritism. But a leader who treats everyone the same will also find it difficult to reward or differentiate others with extra acknowledgment or attention. And then there is the human side: leaders need people they can trust and be comfortable with in order to let their guard down once in a while and generate authentic discussions. Without favorites, who would those people be? Randomly selected employees?

Let's look at the flip side, from the employee's point of view. Isn't it strange how we denigrate people in organizations who actively try to coddle those above them and become a favorite? Yet at the same time, we also see great value in young leaders' seeking out mentors. Mentors are supposed to provide inside advice and perspective. But we all know that having a mentor gives a young leader someone higher up who will speak for him or her in the inner circle. In other words, mentorship is organized favoritism. I say, let favoritism be the coin of exchange in the marketplace of meritocracy.

Choosing a Successor

No one wants to die or even acknowledge that death is inevitable. Yet we expect leaders to plan for their own deaths in a sense and even pick the person who will replace them. The inevitable feeling of threat, the leader's fear that his or her position will be undermined, is entirely natural, and perhaps factual. Why then are we surprised when leaders struggle with choosing a successor?

Until we can acknowledge the complicated emotions that underpin the succession question, we can't hope to manage it effectively. It's difficult for leaders to be open about misgivings around succession. Inevitably others will see that anxiety as being small-minded or self-concerned. But without being able to discuss such concerns, how can we hope to have honest, strategic discussions about the issue?

In this matter, as in many others, having an inner circle can make a critical difference for a leader. Not only could trusted associates provide a sympathetic ear, but they could also support the leader publicly about succession difficulties and deflect some of the heat.

Work-Life Balance

Do leaders have a responsibility to be positive role models for work-life balance? Many leaders don't think so. They'd come to work even if they weren't being paid to do it. They tackle every problem and jump on every issue as if there's no tomorrow. They have no concept of time or the boundary between work and personal life. Some go so far as to demand that same approach from others in the organization. How dare they?

As an organizational challenge, work-life balance seems to be an issue only when expectations aren't clear. In a driven, macho, profit-focused culture like Goldman Sachs, I have never seen people work harder, and I have never heard people complain less about the lack of balance in their lives. Instead, work-life balance seems to be a problem in places where expectations aren't so up-front. As the new science of happiness is showing, satisfaction and contentment are subjective measures. Few leaders have balance in their lives. People don't miss something they don't expect. Similarly, a leader not expecting balance won't miss it. Potential leaders should be aware that the consequences of striving for balance might mean less promotion.

Blatant Self-Interest

Periodically the pendulum swings to another extreme. The rage in corporate self-help now is a call for organizations to do good and be a force for positive social consciousness. Similarly, leaders should not be fixed on their own agendas, but should be "servants" of others.

You'd swear that corporations were cancers on society if you took the news reporting seriously. The dominant view has become that corporations, and leaders, can be forces for good in spite of their natures, not because of them.

It sounds good in theory, so long as you forget three hundred years of capitalism. What great company ever arose without the needs of one individual dominating the needs of many other people? How did our society become so wealthy, rich in goods and services, not to mention jobs and scientific progress, except through the corporate pursuit of profit and market share?

Can leaders talk about such things openly? Not without looking insensitive. I will applaud the first executive who stands up.

Loneliness at the Top

Can leaders be open about their feelings and vulnerabilities? It's more difficult than most people realize. Every mood and move of a CEO is scrutinized microscopically, and the read on that affects the moods and actions of many other people. The strain of such self-control and poise can be quite a challenge to the psyche, not to mention the physical body.

Shouldn't potential leaders know more about this before they get to the top? In turn, wouldn't it be helpful for the organization if the people knew that the leader was human too? When a CEO goes down in scandal or is made vulnerable by a personal failing, many of us enjoy the schadenfreude of the moment. In my experience, most other executives think, "Too bad he got caught. Could have been me." They know that public perfection is a strain that belies human nature. They also know they can't talk about that openly.

DILUTING THE POWER OF TABOOS

How you use the knowledge you have gained about taboos is up to you. In that sense, this has not been a prescriptive book but a descriptive one. It is my belief, however, that good prescriptions come from good descriptions.

Let's look at where taboos come from. Therapists and coaches often use a similar model to the one in Table 12.1 to help individuals identify what they know and what they don't know. This matrix also provides a perspective as to where taboos exist.

There are certain things about an organization that are known to employees in an organization and known to the

Table 12.1. Leadership Awareness Matrix

	Characteristics/ Behaviors Known to Others	Characteristics/ Behaviors Unknown to Others
Characteristics/Behaviors Known to Leader	Public areas	Leadership taboos
Characteristics/Behaviors Unknown to Leader	Leadership blind spots	Subconscious/ potential taboos

leader too. This is organizational or public awareness. There are other things about an organization that are known to everyone but the leader; these are called leadership blind spots. We all know how serious blind spots can be. For some leaders, they're fatal. There are other areas that nobody is aware of, and sometimes an outsider is needed to surface, which could result in potentially new taboos. And then there is that segment of things that leaders know about but no one else in the organization has any idea that they even exist. I believe that leadership taboos fall into this bucket. Taboos are a subset of the knowledge that leaders have that no one else shares (except perhaps other leaders). One of the goals of coaching or therapy is to shrink a person's blind spots so that he or she can be more aware or intentional in life and work. One of the goals of this book is to shrink the territory of leadership taboos so that leaders and followers can be more open and candid about what it really takes to lead—in a sense, to enlarge the public area.

Taboos are electrifying. We can reduce some of their power by first understanding and openly acknowledging that they exist. But just as it is easier to watch reality TV than it is to engage in outlandish reality-based situations, so it is easier to read about taboos than to begin blasting them out of existence at every turn.

Having the privilege to consult for McKinsey & Company for a number of years, I saw firsthand that this firm has the greatest problem solvers in the world. From them, I learned that no one knows how to solve a large, complex problem from the outset. Sure, we all have theories about how a problem can be tackled, but that doesn't mean our theory will work. Because taboos are so emotionally charged and powerful, I recommend that you follow McKinsey's approach to problem solving: develop a hypothesis, test that hypothesis in a limited situation, and expand the experiment if it works.

In other words, if you come across a taboo in your work situation, consider its positives and negatives. Is the existence of the taboo hurting the organization, or does it serve a useful purpose? If the taboo is negative, strategize about the best way to deal with it. More often than not, dealing with a taboo means talking about it openly and beginning a dialogue in which people discuss and debate. Do so on a small scale first, in order to limit the danger of "friendly fire." Prepare for the possibility that emotions will be strong and talk will be heated. But if the discussion leads to a consensus that improves the situation, set up those laboratory conditions in other parts of the organization. Eventually you will find that the dialogue of taboo busting will expand with an energy of its own.

We all know what that feels like. Growing up, we encounter many taboos as children that lose their power when we become adults. Alcohol, drugs, smoking, and sex can be taboos—and very worthy ones for a parent to maintain. The hypercharged feelings of stress and anxiety that are created as a taboo gets approached often dissipate once the taboo has been broken. As we get older, we wonder what happened to the power. If we're lucky, we've moved on, taking the once-illicit act or substance as something we can freely choose to do or choose to avoid in a mature and enlightened way. So it is with organizations and societies. Childhood has many wonders, but becoming an adult has benefits too. If taboos are holding our organizations and leaders down, they should be pruned back or weeded out, allowing our organizations and leaders to grow.

REFERENCES

Argyris, C. "Double Loop Learning in Organizations." *Harvard Business Review,* 1977, *55*(5), 115–125.

"Backlash Against CEOs Could Go Too Far." *Wall Street Journal,* June 15, 2005.

Becker, E. *The Denial of Death.* New York: Free Press, 1973.

Bossidy, L., and Charan, R. *Confronting Reality: Doing What Matters to Get Things Right.* New York: Crown, 2004.

Buchanan, L. "Breakthrough Ideas for 2005." *Harvard Business Review,* Feb. 2005, pp. 17–54.

Burns, J. M. *Leadership.* New York: HarperCollins, 1978.

Charan, R., and Unseem, J. "Why Companies Fail." *Fortune Magazine,* May 27, 2002, pp. 47–58.

Collins, J. *Good to Great.* New York: HarperCollins, 2001.

Collins, J., and Porras, J. *Built to Last.* New York: HarperCollins, 1997.

Covey, S. *The Eighth Habit: From Effectiveness to Greatness.* New York: Free Press, 2004.

Deal, T., and Kennedy, A. *Corporate Cultures: The Rites and Rituals of Corporate Life.* Reading, Mass.: Addison-Wesley, 1982.

de Bono, E. *The Six Thinking Hats.* New York: Little, Brown, 1999.

Deutsch, C. "Behind the Exodus of Executive Women: Boredom." *New York Times,* May 1, 2005.

Farrell, W. *Why Men Earn More.* New York: AMACOM, 2005.

Gartner, J. *The Hypomanic Edge: The Link Between (a Little) Craziness and (a Lot of) Success in America.* New York: Simon & Schuster, 2005.

Goleman, D. *Emotional Intelligence.* New York: Bantam Books. 2005.

Hackman, L., and Porter, L. W. *More About Perspectives on Behavior in Organizations.* New York: McGraw-Hill, 1977.

Hymowitz, C. "Too Many Women Fall for Stereotypes of Selves, Study Says." *Wall Street Journal,* Oct. 24, 2005, p. B1.

Kellerman, B. *Bad Leadership.* Boston: Harvard Business School Press, 2004.

Kerr, S. "On the Folly of Rewarding A, While Hoping for B." *Academy of Management Journal,* Dec. 1975, pp. 769–783.

Mintzberg, H. *Mintzberg on Management.* New York: Free Press, 1989.

Peters, T., and Waterman, R. *In Search of Excellence.* New York: HarperCollins, 1982.

Rost, J. *Leadership for the Twenty-First Century.* New York: Praeger, 1991.

Samuelson, R. J. "No Joke: CEO's Do Some Good." *Newsweek,* Apr. 18, 2005, p. 49.

Sheehy, G. *New Passages: Mapping Your Life Across Time.* New York: Random House, 1995.

Stechart, K. *Sweet Success: How to Understand the Men in Your Business Life—and Win with Your Own Rules.* New York: Macmillan, 1986.

Stewart, J. B. *Disney War.* New York: Simon & Schuster, 2005.

Thomas, D. "Do Not Go Gentle into That Good Night." In A. W. Allison and others (eds.), *The Norton Anthology of Poetry.* (3rd ed.) New York: Norton, 1983.

Welch, J., and Welch, S. *Winning.* New York: HarperCollins, 2005.

Zaleznik, A. *The Managerial Mystique: Restoring Leadership in Business.* New York: HarperCollins, 1989.

ANTHONY SMITH is cofounder and a managing director of Leadership Research Institute, recognized as one of the leading management consulting firms specializing in leadership development and assessment. He has been an active coach and consultant for over twenty years in the areas of organizational change and assessment, team building, executive development, and leadership training and design. He has served clients in a variety of fields, including McKinsey & Company, American Express, the National Football League, the Coca-Cola Company, General Electric, the National Geographic Society, Seimens AG, the Walt Disney Company, ESPN, Deutsche Bank, Spencer Stuart, and Goldman, Sachs and Co.

Smith has served on the teaching and research faculties of several universities, including the University of California and the Tuck School of Business at Dartmouth, and he received a Visiting Professorship at the prestigious EAP Graduate School (European School of Management) at Oxford. He holds a B.A. and M.A. in the behavioral sciences and earned his doctorate from the School of Leadership and Education Sciences at the University of San Diego. Following his doctorate, he was appointed a postdoctoral fellow of social anthropology at the University of California, where he studied leadership and cultural change. His research on leadership has appeared in several publications, including the *European Journal of Management,* the *Journal of Leadership Studies,* and the best-selling books, *The Leader of the Future* and *The Organization of the Future,* both published by Jossey-Bass for the Drucker Foundation. He serves on several boards, including the V Foundation for Cancer Research. The author can be reached through www.taboosofleadership.com and www.dranthonyfsmith.com.

INDEX

A

addiction of leadership, 130–132, 135–136

AIG, 31

Allen, Paul, 77

ambition
  balance vs., 107
  drive required for success, 106, 109–110

American Express, 69, 76

anxiety of breaking taboos, 139–140

Apple, 5

Apprentice, The, 109

Argyris, Chris, 23

Ash, Mary Kay, 5

B

"Backlash Against CEOs Could Go Too Far" (*Wall Street Journal*), 10

Bad Leadership (Kellerman), 6, 121

balance. *See* work-life balance

Becker, Ernest, 110

behavioralism, 16–17

Berkshire Hathaway, 5, 33

Bill and Melinda Gates Foundation, 125

biological characteristics
  identifying with leader's, 34
  leaders', 33–34

blatant self-interest
  ethical dilemmas and, 121–124
  leaders and, 26
  passion as, 127–128
  philanthropy and, 124–127
  taboos against, 120, 149

blind spots, 150, 151

Bodenheimer, George, 32

Booz Allen Hamilton, 62

Bossidy, Larry, 5, 140

Branson, Richard, 4–5, 33

Buchanan, L., 8, 140

Buffett, Warren, 5, 33, 125

Built to Last (Collins and Porras), 18–19

Burns, James MacGregor, 4, 13

Bush, George W., 63, 70, 119, 127, 135

businesses. *See* organizations

C

Campollo, Anthony, 6

care, 22

Carter, Jimmy, 126
CEOs. *See* leaders
character, 22
Charan, Ram, 140, 145
charisma, 31–34
    amplifying perceived power
        with, 50
    biological norms of leaders,
        33–34
    combining skill with, 38–39
    dark side of, 31–32
    leaders known for, 33
    mystique and, 35–42
    myths of, 23
    talking about, 143–144
Cheney, Dick, 63
Churchill, Winston, 33, 39
Clark, Jim, 77, 78
Clinton, Bill, 119, 135
Coca-Cola, 5
coercive power, 49
Collins, Jim, 18–19, 31–32, 40
Comcast, 84
competence, 23
composure, 23
Confronting Reality (Bossidy and
    Charan), 140
contradictions of work-life balance,
    109–112
conviction, 22
Corporate Cultures (Deal and
    Kennedy), 18
corporations. *See* organizations
courage, 22
Covey, Stephen, 127
credibility
    doubts of leader's, 96
    effect of double standard on, 80
    leader's work-life balance and,
        116–117
    six dimensions of, 22–23

crises accentuating loneliness, 136
cultivating loneliness, 133–134

D

de Bono, Edward, 60
Deal, Terrence, 18
death
    fears about, 110
    succession and emotions about,
        93, 101, 147–148
Dell, Michael, 5
Deloitte & Touche, 62
Denial of Death, The, 110
difficulties facing taboos, 140–141
Diller, Barry, 100
diluting power of taboos, 141,
    150–152
Disney, 99–100, 101
double standard, 69–80
    acknowledging costs/benefits of,
        78–80, 145–146
    CEO views on, 74–78
    denying, 69–71
    effect on credibility, 80
    executives breaking taboo of,
        71–74
    downplaying elitism, 70–71
Drucker, Peter, 46, 79

E

effectiveness
    evaluating work-life balance and,
        115
    idealized expectations vs. leader-
        ship, 11
    leadership excellence theories
        and, 18–19
    women leaders and gender bias,
        23–24
Eighth Habit, The (Covey), 127
Eisner, Jane, 100

Eisner, Michael, 99–100
elitism
    acknowledging existence of,
        78–79
    denying double standard, 69–71
    downplaying, 70–71
Ellison, Larry, 77
emotional intelligence, 60–61
emotions
    accepted in workplace, 63
    balancing emotional health, 112–
        113
    charge surrounding taboos, 139–
        140, 152
    hidden conflict within leaders,
        11
    volatility when planning succes-
        sors, 91–93, 101, 147–148
employees. *See also* favoritism
    actions toward, 122–123
    awareness of taboos by, 150–151
    competition for, 51
    difficulties understanding leaders,
        134–135, 142
    disdain for politicians, 43–44
    drive in leaders vs., 133
    family and friends as, 84–86
    getting most from, 117, 128
    identifying with leaders, 34
    imbalances in work lives of, 26,
        107–109
    investment in organization, 133
    looking for dissimilarities in
        leaders, 34–35
    projecting job-related guilt on
        leaders, 111
    weighing benefits of work, 111,
        113–114
Enron, 31, 32, 84, 121
Ernst & Young, 62
ESPN, 123

ethics
    ethical dilemmas and self-
        interest, 121–124
    successful organizations and,
        121–124, 128
    violations and taboos around, 121
executive coaches, 20–22
executives. *See* leaders
expert power, 49–50

F
facilitators, leaders as, 36
family and friends. *See also* favoritism
    dynamics of favoritism, 81–83
    firing, 88
    leaders' views of, 84–86
    protecting leaders who hire, 90
Farrell, Warren, 61–62
favoritism, 81–90
    acknowledging, 89–90, 146–147
    dangers of, 87–89
    dynamics of, 81–83
    meritocracies vs., 25, 82
    motivation and rationale for,
        84–87
    politics and, 86
    protecting leaders who practice,
        90
    reliance on, 83–87
feminine structure of organizations,
    58–59, 63–65
Fidelity, 84
firing family and friends, 88
Fisher, Eileen, 124
followers. *See* employees
Ford, 16
function of taboos, 8

G
gamesmanship. *See* politics
Gartner, John, 110

Gates, Bill, 5, 39, 125, 126
GE, 5, 16, 62, 73–74, 97–99, 107
gender bias. *See also* women leaders
 acknowledging taboos of, 65–66,
 144–145
 women leaders and, 23–24, 55–56
generativity, 86–87, 124–125
Gere, Richard, 53
Gerstner, Lou, 5
GM, 114
Goizueta, Roberto, 5
Goldman Sachs, 114, 148
Goleman, Daniel, 61
Golub, Harvey, 69
Good to Great (Collins), 31–32
Goodell, Roger, 132
Grasso, Dick, 72–73
group theory, 16

H
Harpo Enterprises, 125
health of leaders, 107, 112–113, 129
Hemingway, Ernest, 64
hierarchical authority, 8–9
history of leadership, 15–20
 behavioralism in, 16–17
 group theory, 16
 leadership excellence theories,
 18–19
situational leadership theory, 17–18
Hitler, Adolf, 31
homophily, 34, 50
Honeywell International, 5
Hymowitz, Carol, 62
hypomania, 110
Hypomanic Edge, The (Gartner), 110

I
IBM, 5, 62
idealized expectations of leaders, 11
identifying with leaders, 34
Iger, Robert, 100

Immelt, Jeffrey, 5, 98, 99
In Search of Excellence (Peters and
 Waterman), 18
influence
 credibility and, 22–23
 political power and, 48–50
 integrity and politics, 53

J
Jobs, Steven, 5
Johnson, Ned, 84

K
Karpov, Anatoly, 135
Kasparov, Garry, 135
Keilty, Joe, 44
Kelleher, Herb, 5, 33, 39, 122–123
Kellerman, Barbara, 6, 121, 128
Kennedy, Alan, 18
Kennedy, John F., 39–40
Kerr, Steve, 63–64
Kerry, John, 70, 119
King Jr., Martin Luther, 33
Kozlowski, Dennis, 121

L
leaders. *See also* salaries
 accessibility of, 23
 accusations of unbalanced lives,
 26, 106–109, 112–116
 acknowledging favoritism, 89–
 90, 146–147
 awareness of taboos by, 150–151
 breaking double standard taboo,
 71–74
 CEO views on double standard,
 74–78
 changing spheres of influence,
 125–126
 charismatic, 33–34
 clarifying expectations about
 balance, 114–115, 148

combining skill and charisma, 38–39
dangers of favoritism, 87–89
difficulties being understood, 134–135, 142
disclosing taboos to prepare potential, 10–11
drive vs. balance for successful, 107
empowering others, 83–86
evolution of women's role as, 56–58
executive coaches' views of, 20–22
family and friends viewed by, 84–86
finding key differences in, 34–35
giving up power to others, 94, 101
helping to deal with leadership, 20–21
hidden conflict within, 11
identifying their successor, 25
identifying with, 34
leadership addictions of, 130–132, 135–136
Level 5, 32–33, 40
loneliness of, 129–130, 136–137, 149–150
loyalty and success of, 122–123
modes of relaxation for, 110, 111
motivations driving, 26–27
passion as self-interest, 127–128
pay and perks for, 71–72
personal characteristics of, 19
philanthropy by, 124–127
reluctance to discuss leadership, 13–14
secrets of success unknown, 4–6
self-interest vs. organizational servants, 26
stressing humble origins, 70–71
taboos against position for, 24–25

transitioning to successors, 97–100
viewing from behavioralism focus, 16–17
what it takes to be, 142–143
leadership. See also history of leadership; process of leadership
addictive nature of, 130–132, 135–136
charisma's role in, 33–34
combining skill and charisma in, 38–39
credibility and influence, 22–23
effectiveness vs. idealized expectations, 11
efforts to define, 3–4
enthusiasm for work, 132–133
examining taboos of, 8–12
executive coaches' views of, 20–22
getting most from employees, 117, 128
history of, 15–20
leaders' reluctance to discuss, 13–14
loneliness of, 129–130, 136–137, 149–150
messiness of, 21, 27
model of, 36–38
mystique factor in, 35–40
necessity of politics in, 44–45, 51–54, 144
negative side of politics in, 45–48, 51–54
popular views of, 4
process-oriented approach to, 21–22
styles of male and female, 62
theory vs. practice in, 23–24
transactional vs. transformational, 111, 113–114
turning over to successors, 96–97

leadership, *continued*
    understanding, 13–15, 19–20
    what it takes for, 142–143
    women's will for, 61–62, 65–66,
        145
Leadership Awareness Matrix, 150
leadership excellence theories, 18–19
Leadership (MacGregor), 4
leadership succession. *See* successors
Level 5 leaders, 32–33, 40
loneliness of leadership
    accentuated by crises, 136
    cultivating, 133–134
    enthusiasm for work and, 132–133
    need to be understood, 134–135,
        142
    taboo of acknowledging, 129–
        130, 136–137, 149–150
Louis XIV, 91–92
loyalty and success of leaders, 122–123
LRI, 22, 55

M

Managerial Mystique, The (Zaleznick),
    40–41
Manson, Charles, 31
Mary Kay Cosmetics, 5
McKinsey & Co., 115–116, 121,
    151–152
men
    adapting skills to emotional
        intelligence, 60
    effect of women on, 57–58, 59
    leadership styles of women and,
        62
mentorship, 147
meritocracies, 25, 82, 146
messiness of leadership, 21, 27
Mickelson, Phil, 106
Microsoft, 5, 77
Mintzberg, Henry, 46–48, 49
Mother Teresa, 33, 126

motivation
    leader's behavior as, 37
    understanding leader's, 26–27
Multifactor Leadership Model, 36–
    38
Murdoch, Rupert, 83–84
mystic behavior, 37
mystique
    manufacturing, 40–42
    talking about charisma and, 143–
        144
    understanding leadership, 35–40
myths
    charisma, 23
    hiding taboos with, 6

N

Napoleon, 17
National Football League, 114, 132
nepotism. *See also* favoritism
    denial of, 83
    motivation and rationale for, 84–
        87
Netscape, 77
New Passages (Sheehy), 86–87, 124–
    125
New York Stock Exchange (NYSE),
    72
Newscorp, 83
Nicholson, Jack, 145
Nicklaus, Jack, 105
Nicole, 134–135
Nike, 76, 106, 109
Nixon, Richard, 39–40
"No Joke: CEO's Do Some Good"
    (Samuelson), 128

O

"On the Folly of Rewarding A,
    While Hoping for B" (Kerr),
    63–64
O'Neill, Paul, 26

optimal heterophylly, 34–35
Oracle, 77
organizations
    cultural taboos of, 7
    dominated by politics, 43–44
    effect of leadership charisma on, 32
    ethics and values in successful, 121–124, 128
    executive and workers' salary ratios, 79
    failures of, 140
    feminine skills needed in flattened, 58–59
    leaders as servants of, 26
    male focus of, 63–65
    meritocracies vs. favoritism in, 25, 82
    past purposes served by taboos, 142
    politics as illness in, 46–48
    results of charismatic leaders, 42
    taboo of favoritism in, 81–83
    testing work-life balance of, 116
    types of power in, 49–50
    value-based, 18–19
outcomes in situational leadership, 18
Ovitz, Michael, 99, 100

P
passion
    self-interest and, 127
    work as leader's, 132–133
perceived power, 50
perks, 71–72
personal characteristics of leader, 19
Peters, Tom, 18
Pfizer, 115
philanthropists, 124–127
politics, 43–54
    accessibility of leaders vs., 23
    acknowledging existence of, 9–10, 144
    competition for followers in, 51
    defined, 50
    disdain for, 43–44
    favoritism and, 86
    gamesmanship in, 46–47
    integrity and, 53
    leadership taboo of, 44–45
    mode of power and influence, 48–50
    necessity of, 44–45, 51–54, 144
    negative side of, 45–48, 51–54
    organizational illness and, 46–48
Porras, Larry, 18–19
Power, 53
power. *See also* salaries
    changing spheres of influence, 125–126
    favorite's use of, 87–88
    giving up when empowering others, 94
    politics as mode of, 48–50
    power of taboos, 7
    signified by salaries, 71–72, 77
    types of organizational, 49–50
pragmatic behavior, 36
process of leadership
    helping leaders deal with, 20–21
    messiness in, 21, 27
    politics in, 48–50
    understanding, 13–15
Procter & Gamble, 62
Professional Golf Association, 105

Q
Quattrone, Frank, 121

R
Reagan, Ronald, 33, 119
reciprocity, 122
referent power, 50

Roberts, Brian, 84
Roberts, Julia, 74–75, 77
Rockefeller, John D., 99
Roosevelt, Franklin D., 45
Rost, Joseph, 15

S

salaries
    executive, 70, 74–78
    executive and workers', 79
    power signified by, 71–72, 77
Samuelson, Robert J., 128
servant leadership, 120
Sheehy, Gail, 86–87, 124–125
Silicon Graphics, 77
situational leadership theory, 17–18
Skilling, Jeffrey, 5, 121
Soros, George, 125, 126
Southwest Airlines, 5, 33, 39, 122
Sporting News, 32
Standard Oil, 99
Stechart, Kathryn, 49–50
Stewart, James, 99
Stewart, Martha, 5, 121
success
    blatant self-interest and, 128, 149
    drive required for, 106, 109–110
    drive vs. balance, 107
successors
    difficulties identifying, 25, 91–
        93
    emotions involved in planning,
        91–93, 101, 147–148
    empowering others, 83–86
    favoritism in choosing, 86–87
    letting go to, 96–97
    transitioning to new, 97–100
Summers, Larry, 65, 145

T

"Taboo on Taboos, A" (Buchanan), 8

taboos. *See also* taboos of person;
    taboos of persuasion; taboos of
    position
    acknowledging loneliness, 129–
        130, 136–137, 149–150
    admitting existence of, 9–10
    against organizational position,
        24–25
    blatant self-interest as, 120, 149
    dark side of charisma, 31–32
    defined, 6
    difficulties facing, 140–141
    diluting power of, 141, 150–152
    emotional charge of, 139–140,
        152
    ethics violations and, 121
    favoritism, 81–83, 89–90, 146–147
    function of, 8
    grooming successors, 25, 91–93
    hiding within myths, 6–7
    leaders' reluctance to discuss
        leadership, 13–14
    living unbalanced life, 106–109
    organizational, 7
    past purposes served by, 142
    politics, 44–45
    power of, 7
    preparing potential leaders by
        disclosing, 10–11
    reason for examining, 8–12
    strategies for dealing with, 152
taboos of person. *See also* blatant
    self-interest; loneliness of
    leadership; work-life balance
    about, 25–27
    accusations of unbalanced lives,
        106–109
    acknowledging loneliness, 129–
        130, 136–137, 149–150
    taboos against blatant self-
        interest, 120, 149

taboos of persuasion. *See also*
charisma; politics; women leaders
acknowledging gender taboos
and biases, 23–24, 55–56,
65–66
charisma and leadership, 31–34
factors in taboos of, 22–24
manufacturing mystique, 40–42
mystique in leadership, 35–40
necessity of politics, 44–45, 51–54
taboos of position. *See also* double
standard; favoritism; successors
costs/benefits of double standard,
78–80, 145–146
denial of double standard, 69–71
difficulties identifying successors,
25, 91–93
executives breaking double
standard taboos, 71–74
favoritism, 81–83, 89–90, 146–147
taboos of, 24–25
women as better leaders, 23–24,
55–56, 144–145
Tagliabue, Paul, 5, 132
teaching behavior, 36
team leadership, 16
testing hypotheses, 151–152
Thomas, Dylan, 101
transactional leadership, 111
transformational leadership, 111, 113
Trump, Donald, 5, 109
Trump Organization, 5
Tyco, 31, 121

U
Unseem, Jerry, 140, 145

V
values. *See also* ethics
combining business with other,
124

effects on leadership, 119–120
organizations based on, 18–19
Virgin, 4–5, 33
visionaries, leader's behaviors as, 37

W
Wall Street, 120
Wal-Mart, 5, 69–70
Walters, Barbara, 31
Walton, Sam, 5
Washington, George, 17
Waterman, Robert, 18
Watson, Tom, 5
Welch, Jack, 5, 33, 73–74, 97–99,
107, 116–117
Welch, Suzy, 117
Wells, Frank, 100
Whitman, Meg, 5
"Why Companies Fail" (Charan and
Unseem), 145
Why Men Earn More (Farrell), 61–62
Winfrey, Oprah, 125
Winning (Welch and Welch), 117
women leaders
acknowledging gender taboos,
23–24, 55–56, 65–66, 144–145
attrition of, 61–63
effect on men in workplace, 57–
58
emotional intelligence of, 60–61
evolution of, 56–58
preference for male bosses and
reports, 55, 63
skills in flattened organizations,
58–59
underlying male focus of organizations, 63–65
will for leadership, 61–62, 65–66,
145
work-life balance and, 62, 107–
108

Woods, Tiger, 75, 76, 105–106, 109, 111–112
work-life balance
  accusations of imbalanced lives, 106–109
  clarifying expectations of, 114–115, 148
  contradictions of, 109–112

conundrum for leaders, 25–27
credibility in leader's, 116–117
facing accusations about, 112–116
Tiger Woods and, 105–106
women and, 62, 107–108

Z

Zaleznick, Abraham, 40